WEST INDIAN READERS

BOOK FOUR

NELSON'S

WEST INDIAN READERS

Book FOUR

Compiled by J. O. Cutteridge

OXFORD
UNIVERSITY PRESS

Great Clarendon Street, Oxford, OX2 6DP, United Kingdom

Oxford University Press is a department of the University of Oxford. It furthers the University's objective of excellence in research, scholarship, and education by publishing worldwide. Oxford is a registered trade mark of Oxford University Press in the UK and in certain other countries

First published by Thomas Nelson and Sons in 1926
Second edition published by Nelson Thornes Ltd in 2013
This edition published by Oxford University Press in 2014

British Library Cataloguing in Publication Data
Data available

978-1-4085-2355-1

4

Printed and bound by CPI Group (UK) Ltd, Croydon, CR0 4YY

Acknowledgements

Page make-up: Compuscript Ltd

Although we have made every effort to trace and contact all copyright holders before publication this has not been possible in all cases. If notified, the publisher will rectify any errors or omissions at the earliest opportunity.

PREFATORY NOTE FOR TEACHERS

THIS Book follows the plan of its predecessors, and at the same time introduces two new features:

i. *Picture Lessons.*—Reproductions of some of the world's best pictures are included. The accompanying lessons will help the pupils to study pictures with an appreciation similar to that which is aroused by the proper study of literature.

ii. *History.*—An attempt has been made to bring together the apparently disconnected events in the early days of the respective West Indian colonies into a more or less continuous narrative. Through the medium of the historical lessons in this and the following book, the pupils will gain a knowledge of an outline of the history of the West Indies as a whole, and thus prepare a setting for the more detailed study of their own particular colony.

The literature given in this Book should be supplemented by the following books:

1. *Monte Cristo.* Parts I. and II. Nelson's Classics School Edition.
2. *Folk-Tales of the Nations.* Nelson's "Teaching of English" Series.
3. *Tom Brown's Schooldays.* Nelson's Classics School Edition.
4. *Treasure Island.* Nelson's "Teaching of English" Series.
5. *The Talisman.* Nelson's "Historical Romances" Series, or Nelson's Classics.
6. *The Story of Columbus.* Nelson's "Children's Heroes" Series.
7. *Sir Walter Raleigh.* Nelson's "Teaching of English" Series.

I am again indebted to Dr. J. R. Dickson, Deputy Surgeon-General, Trinidad, for assistance with the hygiene lessons; to Mr. R. O. Williams for help in the preparation of the lessons on Nature Study; to Mr. G. H. A. Bunyan for the lesson on Guyana to Mr. F. W. Reeves, M.A., for the lesson on Arrowroot; to Mr. T. Spencer for many of the local drawings; and to The New Trinidad Lake Asphalt Company and Mr. C. Phelps for photographs for the lesson on "The Wonder Lake of Trinidad." My thanks are also due to Messrs. Cadbury Bros. for the facilities afforded me when visiting their factory at Bournville, and for the photographs they have supplied for the lesson on "Cocoa and Chocolate," as well as to all others who have assisted in any way with the preparation of this Book.

J. O. CUTTERIDGE.

Acknowledgements

The author and the publisher would also like to thank the following for permission to reproduce material:

Images
p19: Aberdeen Art Gallery & Museum Collections; p23: Portrait of Napoleon I (1769–1821), 1815 (oil on canvas), Vernet, Antoine Charles Horace (Carle) (1758–1836)/National Gallery, London, UK/ The Bridgeman Art Library; p32: Antiquarian Images/Mary Evans Picture Library; p38: National Gallery/AKG-Images; p47: UIG/Getty Images; p51: Patrick Robert/Sygma/Corbis; p55: The Hay Wain, 1821 (oil on canvas), Constable, John (1776–1837)/National Gallery, London, UK/The Bridgeman Art Library; p58: Stewart; p75: The Concert: Singer and Theorbo Player (oil on panel), Borch or Terborch, Gerard ter (1617–81)/Louvre, Paris, France/Giraudon/The Bridgeman Art Library; p78: Windsor Castle, Lydon, Alexander Francis (1836–1917)/Private Collection/© Look and Learn/ The Bridgeman Art Library; p80: Pictorial Press/Alamy; p81: Justin Kase/Alamy; p83: Micro Stock Images/Alamy; p85: Dan Breckwoldt/Shutterstock; p95: An Alchemist, 1611 (oil on oak), Ostade, Adriaen Jansz. van (1610–85)/National Gallery, London, UK/The Bridgeman Art Library; p120: Queen Elizabeth, Sir Francis Drake and knights on the deck of the Golden Hind (colour litho), Huens, Jean-Leon (1921–82)/National Geographic Creative/The Bridgeman Art Library; p131: A Lonely Life, c.1873, Cameron, Hugh (1835–1918)/© Scottish National Gallery, Edinburgh/The Bridgeman Art Library; pp132–133, 137: Cadbury Brothers Ltd; p149: Glasgow Art Gallery; p168: The Avenue at Middelharnis, 1689 (oil on canvas), Hobbema, Meindert (1638–1709)/National Gallery, London, UK/The Bridgeman Art Library; p185: Time Watch Images/Alamy; pp189–193: Trinidad Asphalt Company Ltd; p204: J. R. Skelton; p206: Interfoto Sammlung Rauch/Mary Evans Picture Library; p211: Anne Bolt; p221: The Sheepfold, Moonlight, 1856–60 (oil on panel), Millet, Jean-Francois (1814–75)/© Walters Art Museum, Baltimore, USA/The Bridgeman Art Library; p225: Tim Laman/ Getty Images; p233: Simon Harmon Vedder; p240: Sir J. Noel Paton.

Every effort has been made to trace the copyright holders but if any have been inadvertently overlooked the publisher will be pleased to make the necessary arrangements at the first opportunity.

CONTENTS

An Asterisk (*) indicates Poetry.

LESSON 1

TOBACCO AND CIGARS

THE West Indies are famous throughout the world for several products, such as Jamaica rum, Trinidad asphalt, St. Vincent arrowroot, and the sea-island cotton from the Leeward Islands, but it is doubtful if any one of these has a greater fame than the cigars made in Cuba and Jamaica. Much tobacco is grown in Virginia in North America for pipe smoking, and in the countries around the Mediterranean, such as Turkey and Egypt, for cigarette making, but the best cigars in the world are made from West Indian tobacco. The "La Tropical" cigars, made in the Machado factory at Kingston, and the "Golofina" cigars of the Jamaica Tobacco Company are known to every cigar smoker in both the New and the Old World.

Most plants are grown for the sake of their fruit, roots, or juices, but, like the tea plant, tobacco is grown solely for its leaves. The plant needs a good deal of care to cultivate it successfully and to produce the large well-formed leaves which are required for cigar making.

Tobacco requires a light soil in a valley or on gently sloping or flat lands, and there is plenty of such land suitable for its growth on the south side of Jamaica in the parishes of St. Andrew, St. Catherine, and Clarendon.

The plant is grown from small seeds, which are first sown in boxes or in specially prepared beds. After about two months the young seedlings are transplanted into the fields, which have previously been well ploughed, and the remains of any plants, such as weeds, that have rotted, well dug in. The young plants should not be put out in dry weather, or they will die. In Jamaica a little manure is usually put into each hole before the seedlings are planted, and the land is heavily mulched.

After a short time the plants have to be moulded up, and then, when a sufficient number of leaves has grown, the tops, side-shoots, and flower-buds are all nipped off in order that the plant may put all its energy of growth into the leaves. These will then develop, and a rich harvest will be reaped provided that a watchful eye is kept on the insect pests which attack this crop as they do all others in tropical countries.

The tobacco growers keep a careful watch on the plantation, not only to detect the plant enemies, but also to report on the varying conditions of each field, as the manufacturers require great uniformity in the leaves. As soon as these are fully grown and turn slightly yellow, they are carefully removed from the stalk and hung in loose bundles in an airy room until they begin to shrivel and turn brown in colour.

The next process, that of fermentation, has to be carried out with extreme care, as certain stages are so delicate, that even if a door were left open in one of the buildings the leaves might become chilled and their value lessened. The leaves are placed evenly upon one another in heaps, and covered with plantain leaves for about a month, being occasionally turned over. This process gives them their well-known flavour in smoking.

They are then tied in bundles, or "hands," of about thirty leaves, packed in boxes or hogsheads, and sent to the factory. On arrival there they are damped in order to render them pliable, stripped of their mid-ribs, and sorted into different grades for cigars and cigarettes.

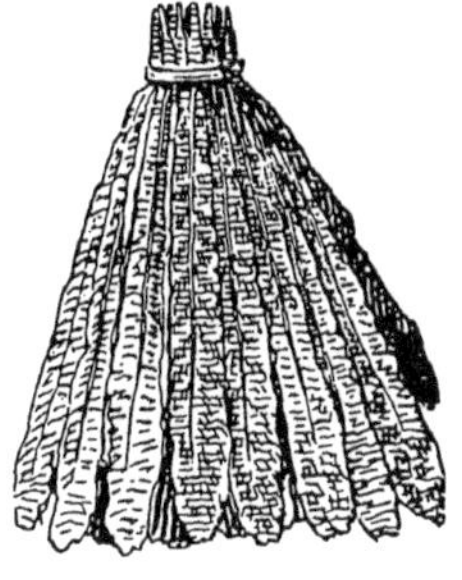

A "Hand."

As you can see in the picture, a cigar consists of a core or central mass of "fillers," wrapped in an inner and an outer covering leaf. The filling is done by hand, and care is required to pack the leaves properly so that the cigar will burn evenly, and that the smoke may be drawn freely from end to end. After the cigar has been properly shaped it is wrapped in its outer cover in a spiral manner, beginning at the thick end and working down to the pointed end. It is then pressed in a mould. Each worker will make about two hundred cigars in a day.

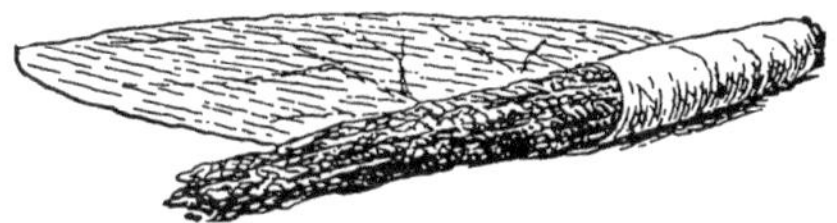

Rolling a Cigar.

In one well-lighted room of the factory facing the north, to avoid the direct rays of the sun, the experts may be seen grading the cigars by their colour. You may have seen these names on the boxes—"Claro," "Colorado Claro," "Colorado," "Colorado Maduro," or

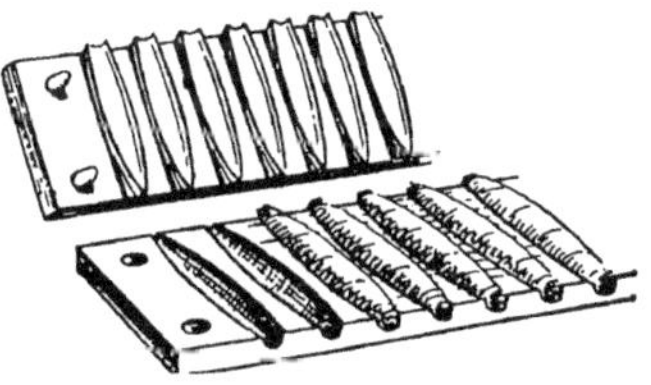

Mould for Cigars.

"Maduro." The last named is the darkest and strongest grade. Finally, the cigars are labelled, pressed, and packed into the dainty cedar-wood boxes with their artistic labels, in which they find their way into all countries of the world, spreading the fame of the West Indies with them.

Exercises

1. The names showing the grades of cigars are Spanish words. One means "mature," or thoroughly ripe; another means "clear"; and another means "red" or "coloured." Study the words, and you will see which they are.
2. Make sentences of your own containing these words:

pliable	vigilance	evenly
experts	uniformity	mould
energy	artistic	dainty
cultivate	spiral	finally

3. Explain the difference between "lessen" and "lesson." What part of speech is each of these words?
4. Fill in the blanks:
   (*a*) The island of —— enjoys a reputation for the —— of tobacco and the manufacture of ——.
   (*b*) Its cigars bear favourable comparison with those —— in the neighbouring island of ——, the largest of the West Indies.
   (*c*) Cuban cigars are usually known as —— cigars, from the capital of the island.
   (*d*) During the Spanish-American War many expert —— makers left Cuba and took up their abode under the —— flag in Jamaica. What was ——'s loss was ——'s gain.

LESSON 2

HOW A PRISONER OF WAR ESCAPED

DURING World War I. King George V. was much interested in those British prisoners of war who managed to escape from Germany. Here is the story of Private R. Woodcock, 1st Royal West Kent Regiment, as he told it to the King at Windsor in May 1916.

"It was at Neuve Chapelle that I was made prisoner. I had gone back to fetch a fellow who had been wounded, when I found myself cut off by the Germans. There was nothing for it but to surrender. The Germans pushed me against a wall, and made signs to me to dig my own grave. I should have been shot if a German officer had not hurried up to my rescue.

"At the beginning of November 1914 I found myself in prison, where I remained for seventeen long, dreary months. It seemed almost hopeless to attempt to escape. But where there's a will there's a way. Our beds were in tiers on the top of each other in a brick building with a thin wall.

"Somebody managed to get possession of tools, and we set to work to make a manhole in the wall. Only one man could work at a time, and he had to lie full length under the lowest of the beds while he chipped away at the wall.

"Every five minutes, when the sentry came in, he had to cease work. The rest of us chatted as if nothing was going on. We hid the displaced bricks in our mattresses, and had to try to sleep upon them.

"After two weeks' hard work the hole was big enough for us to crawl through. Roll call was at 8.30 in the evening, and an hour later we had the last brick out of the wall. Then one of us wormed his way through, and at this moment the German sentry came in. When he went out another of our fellows slipped through, and in came the sentry again. Every time the German went out one man crawled through the hole, until eight of us were in an office on the other side.

"I found a window, which I forced, and before long we were all of us outside the prison. Then we split up into two parties, one of three and the other of five, and away we went. I belonged to the party of five.

"The other party, as I afterwards learned, made a short cut for the frontier, but fell into the hands of the Germans about a mile from the prison. We took a roundabout route and were more fortunate—for a time.

"It was the middle of March, and a great blizzard was blowing. Nearly frozen to death, we crawled through barbed wire, dashed through private estates, fell, got up again, and were off once more. All around us we could hear dogs yelping as they followed our track. The snow was deep on the ground, and we took refuge in a wood about eight miles from the frontier. There we ate the food which we had brought with us.

"All day we lay hidden in the wood, with chattering teeth and numbed limbs. Next night we made for the frontier, but before long we were dead beat. The blizzard was too much for us, and we had to turn into a barn and rest for twelve hours in its loft. We did not know that another mile and a half would have brought us into Holland.

"At ten o'clock in the morning a little girl came into the barn. She ran out again and returned with her brother. He climbed up to the loft, peeped in, saw us, and then ran off like a shot.

"'Come on boys!' I said, 'as quick as you can.'

"There was a drop of sixteen feet to the road, and I took it first. Our luck did not serve us that day. I landed in the middle of a German patrol of three men with rifles. Of course they seized us, and back we were all sent to our prison, to be tried by court-martial for attempting to escape.

"While I was waiting my trial, I made another attempt to escape. This is how I managed it. A party of prisoners was leaving the camp to work at some old forts on the other side of the Rhine. A Belgian named Marcel was one of the party, and he and I agreed to make our escape together. I persuaded one of the English prisoners in the same party to let me change places with him.

"Marcel had managed to smuggle into the prison two suits of civilian clothes, and these we put on under our uniforms. We each had a German cap in our pockets, so we were quite ready to disguise ourselves at the first opportunity.

"Before we had finished our first day's work on the forts, Marcel and I managed to bury our uniform trousers and tunics. This left us in our civilian clothes, which were concealed by our greatcoats.

"At five o'clock we began marching back to camp. There were German soldiers in front of us and German soldiers behind us. I saw that once we were round a bend in the lane the Germans behind would not be able to see us, and the Germans in front would have their backs to us.

"As soon as we turned the bend, off we took our overcoats, and on we put our civilian caps. Then we sprang out of the ranks on to the path and turned right about. We were just in time to meet the German soldiers coming round the corner.

"Marcel had taught me to say 'Good-day' in German, and I now greeted the soldiers in their own tongue. All the time I was quaking in my boots. They replied, and passed on. They had no idea that we were escaped prisoners. We hurried along, and when we turned the corner breathed a big sigh of relief.

"All night we walked on, and next morning found ourselves between two towns which were full of soldiers. We dared not travel by day, so we took refuge in a wood and concealed ourselves amidst the bushes.

"After some hours a party of Germans came into the wood and began collecting sticks, which they tied together into fagots. They worked for a full five hours, and sometimes they were only five paces from our hiding-places. All this time we were growing hungrier and hungrier: we had tasted no morsel of food since we made our escape.

"When at last the Germans left the wood we made a desperate dash for the frontier. We swam rivers, crept along ditches, crawled through barbed wire, slipped through lines of sentries, and played hide-and-seek with cavalry patrols. A dozen times we were within an ace of being captured.

"About two in the morning I said to Marcel, 'How shall we know when we are over the frontier?'

"'The sleepers of the railway in Germany are made of iron,' he replied; 'in Holland they are made of wood.'

"Just then we came on a railway line. 'Wood!' I shouted. 'Thank God, we are in Holland!'

"A few days later I was back in England, a free man once more."

Exercises

1. Give these expressions in another way:
   "nothing for it but."
   "wormed his way through."
   "dead beat."
   "where there's a will there's a way."
2. Give the opposite of these terms:

civilian	cease	roundabout	persuaded
cavalry	dreary	frozen	bury
concealed	captured	hurry	brother

3. Relate any other incident of the World War that you have heard or read of.
4. In what regiment did West Indians serve during the World War?
5. What is the missing letter in each of these words?—

desp*rate	sle*pers	Belg*an	se*zed
sep*rate	disg*ise	R*ine	man*ged
front*er	num*ed	bliz*ard	w*rmed

6. Describe in your own words the escape of Private Woodcock and Marcel the Belgian.
7. Make sentences containing the following words:

smuggle	trial	uniform	disguise
tunic	whipped	quaking	foliage
morsel	stumbled	relief	opportunity

LESSON 3

PICTURE LESSONS—I

Introduction.—In order to appreciate the beauties of art we must study some of the masterpieces in its various branches, and learn to distinguish between the bad and the good, the ugly and the beautiful. Examples of the world's best music can be heard in our homes through the medium of a gramophone, and they are sometimes played by our bands or on the organs in our churches; the best in literature is available for our study in books; but in the West Indies we seldom have the opportunity to see any of the masterpieces painted by great artists. There is an old saying, however, which states "If Mahomet is unable to go to the mountain, then the mountain must be brought to Mahomet." As you are unable to journey to the great Art Galleries of Europe, where many of these masterpieces are housed, I am bringing reproductions of some of them to you in this and the following book, for you to study with the aid of the Picture Lessons which accompany them.

Titian as a Beginner

In the picture on the opposite page we see the youthful Italian artist Titian (1477–1576) making his first attempt at painting.

We are told in a very old book that "when Titian was a little boy he gave the earliest indication of his future fame as a colourist by drawing a Madonna, which he coloured with the juices of flowers."

How carefully the artist has pictured the youthful genius sitting on a chair and looking up thoughtfully at the statue he has been copying!

His drawing-book is lying beside him under his right hand, which clasps a pencil and a bunch of flowers.

TITIAN'S FIRST ATTEMPT IN COLOUR.
(*William Dyce, R. A., 1806–64. By kind permission of the Trustees of the Aberdeen Art Gallery.*)

We see a basket full of bright flowers lying on the grass at his feet. There are red geraniums and tulips, yellow crocuses and primroses, as well as blue hyacinths and irises.* Close at hand may be seen a water-bottle, a sponge, and a painting-cloth.

The whole picture is full of interesting details, while every part of it is painted with the greatest neatness and care.

William Dyce was a Scottish artist who lived about one hundred years ago. He believed that whatever was worth painting was worth painting in careful detail. That is why he gave the same attention and care to the painting of the leaves of the trees, and even the weeds among the grass, as he gave to the painting of the boy and the statue.

Notice the care he has expended upon the trunks of the trees, the blades of the grass, the bamboo stick leaning against the tree stump, as well as upon the boy's face, hands, and clothes.

The general colour of the picture is green, while the boy is dressed in a dark green tunic which shows the sleeves of a yellow undercoat. His hose are black, and his cap of black velvet is lying near the pedestal of the statue.

Many artists both before and after Dyce's time painted the important parts of their pictures carefully, but paid less attention to the unimportant parts. Which do you think is the better kind of picture: the kind which is neatly painted all over, or the kind in which the important parts are carefully painted and the unimportant parts less carefully painted?

This is a difficult question even for grown-up people to answer. If we are open-minded we shall find room in our

* These are all flowers which bloom in the gardens of Europe in the spring.

hearts and minds for both kinds. Each artist tries to give us what is best in him, and if we are willing we may learn many things from all kinds of pictures.

We do not object to poetry because it is not prose, nor to prose because it is not poetry. Both are good, each in its own place, yet both are different. So in painting, the "realist" shows us details he has seen and studied—as Dyce does in this picture. The poet painter or "impressionist"* shows us the chief things which are in his mind; he opens a new door to us and gives us a new vision—a new general impression. Both teach us something of nature and beauty.

LESSON 4

INCIDENT OF THE FRENCH CAMP

Introduction.—Napoleon (the first Emperor of France, whose wife, the Empress Josephine, was born in Martinique) was the famous soldier and statesman whose ambition was to be master of Europe. The poem describes his usual way of standing with his legs apart and his arms folded behind him. Browning also relates in it a real event which happened near Ratisbon, a German town on the Danube, in Napoleon's war with Austria in 1809. The only difference between the poet's account and the actual episode is that the hero was a man.

You know, we French stormed Ratisbon:
  A mile or so away,
On a little mound, Napoleon
  Stood on our storming-day—

* See pages 131 and 221.

With neck out-thrust, you fancy how,
Legs wide, arms locked behind,
As if to balance the prone brow
Oppressive with its mind.

Just as perhaps he mused, "My plans
That soar, to earth may fall,
Let once my army-leader Lannes*
Waver at yonder wall,"
Out 'twixt the battery-smokes there flew
A rider, bound on bound
Full-galloping; nor bridle drew
Until he reached the mound.

Then off there flung in smiling joy,
And held himself erect
By just his horse's mane, a boy;
You hardly could suspect
(So tight he kept his lips compressed,
Scarce any blood came through)—
You looked twice ere you saw his breast
Was all but shot in two.

"Well," cried he, "Emperor, by God's grace
We've got you Ratisbon!
The marshal's in the market-place,
And you'll be there anon
To see your flag-bird flap his vans†
Where I to heart's desire
Perched him!" The chief's eye flashed; his plans
Soared up again like fire.

* One of Napoleon's chief officers.

† Vanes; wings.

NAPOLEON.

The chief's eye flashed, but presently
   Softened itself, as sheathes
A film the mother-eagle's eye
   When her bruised eaglet breathes—
"You're wounded!" "Nay," the soldier's pride
   Touched to the quick, he said,
"I'm killed, sire!" And his chief beside,
   Smiling, the boy fell dead.

ROBERT BROWNING.

EXERCISES

1. Fill in the blanks:
   (*a*) To *storm* a fort or town means to take it by a sudden attack. Another way is by a ——, which often takes a long time. The —— of Troy lasted for ten years.
   (*b*) A lamb is a young sheep; —— is a young eagle.
   (*c*) *Prone* usually means lying —— on the ground; in the poem it merely indicates *drooping*.
   (*d*) *Quick* has several meanings. One of them is that of the sensitive part of the finger-nails which cannot be cut without pain, so that *touched to the quick* means sharply ——.
2. Give an example of alliteration in this poem.
3. What part of speech is each of the following:
   erect, sheathes, quick, soar, marshal, and bruised.
4. *Presently* is often used in the West Indies to mean "at present" or "now." This is incorrect. What does the poet mean by *presently* in this poem?
5. Describe the picture of Napoleon on page 23.
6. Write out in your own words the story of the poem.

LESSON 5

THE HOUSE-FLY

THE house-fly, as the name implies, lives most commonly in or near our houses.

It is found in most countries of the world, but thrives best and is most abundant in tropical countries, for the reason that the high temperature of those countries allows flies to breed throughout the whole year, whereas in cooler climes they sleep during the winter and become active only during the summer.

House-Fly, adult (enlarged).

The fly appears to be the most perfectly free and independent of creatures as it flits in and out of our houses. Its taste in food is peculiar; it feeds with as much relish on the most filthy refuse in our backyards as on the most dainty food or sweetmeat in our houses. This custom gives it special opportunities for spreading certain diseases, and thus it is important that we should have a knowledge of its life history and habits.

Like the mosquito, the fly is hatched from an egg, and passes through the stages of larva, grub or maggot, pupa or chrysalis, and finally becomes the full-grown adult fly.

Horse manure or stable refuse is their favourite breeding-place, but flies will breed in almost any kind of rotten substance, such as human or animal excrement, bad meat, dead animals, decaying vegetables and fruit, rotting straw and leaves, and even in spittoons. They generally lay their eggs on refuse or waste matter in which decay is in progress, as the eggs and grubs require warmth and moisture, and both of these conditions accompany the process of decay.

Larva (enlarged).

A single fly will deposit at one time from a hundred to a hundred and fifty eggs, and in the course of her life may produce six or more batches of this size. The eggs hatch in from twelve to twenty-four hours, and the larvæ appear as small white worms with the body tapering towards the head end, and stout and blunt at the hinder end. You can see this in the picture.

The larva, or maggot, feeds greedily on the moist substance surrounding it, and is very active, constantly burrowing into the soft warm refuse. It is only in this stage that the insect grows, and after changing its skin several times it becomes full grown in about three or four days.

The larva now leaves the moist part of the manure heap and seeks a dry sheltered spot, which it finds, perhaps, by burrowing down into a drier layer of the heap. There it rests, and after keeping quiet for an hour or two it draws in its front end and takes on a barrel-shaped outline, while its white colour slowly changes to a mahogany brown.

It has now entered on the chrysalis or pupa stage. Within the pupa case, which is now a hard skin, the larva undergoes a wonderful change, and in about three or four days the crawling, distasteful maggot is changed into the lively insect that we know as the house-fly. The hard skin of the pupa cracks, and out crawls the adult fly, which stretches its wings, and after a short time flies away.

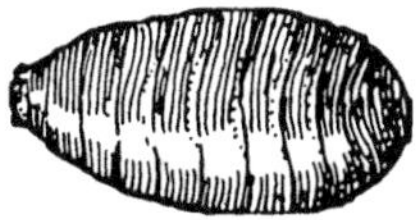

Pupa (enlarged).

The house-fly is not a biting insect, and can only suck up liquid food. When we see it feeding on solid substances, such as sugar or bread, it has dissolved these by depositing saliva on them and is sucking up the liquid so produced. It also frequently vomits food in a drop which it generally sucks back again.

Our particular interest in the fly is due to its importance as a carrier of disease, especially bacterial diseases such as typhoid fever, cholera, dysentery, and diarrhœa. It carries such diseases in a variety of ways. The germs are picked up by the proboscis or trunk, the body and the legs, as the fly feeds on filth. They are also sucked into its stomach.

When feeding, the fly passes out excrement, and as it has been proved that some of the germs sucked in remain alive and are passed out in an active state, it is now thought that this is the most usual way of conveying infection. Experiments have also proved that germs taken in during the larval stage remain alive, and are still active when it becomes an adult fly.

Flies are constantly passing from refuse and filth to our houses, and thus have numerous opportunities of conveying infection directly to the lips or nostrils, or to wounds, and indirectly by soiling food and other objects.

The prevalence of flies is not only a direct menace to health, but is also an indication that yards and premises are not kept clean, but contain decaying refuse. It is not necessary that we should be troubled by swarms of flies, for it is quite easy to control and get rid of them by cleanliness. They can best be suppressed by destroying their breeding-places. This simply means taking care to keep our houses and yards clean. Refuse of all kinds—particularly stable refuse—should be regularly removed, preferably daily, being stored pending removal in boxes or dustbins with well-fitting covers, and safely disposed of by being burnt, dug into gardens, or spread out in low-lying spots and covered over.

Food, whether in private houses or on sale in shops and in the streets, should be protected by glass or wire covers or nets.

There are many methods of dealing with adult flies, such as swatting, trapping, use of sticky papers, and poisoning. These are helpful, but cannot take the place of direct attacks on breeding-places.

Exercises

1. Why is the house-fly classed as an insect?
2. Collect some larvæ (the little white maggots) from a rubbish heap and put them in a glass bottle containing a little sand. Tie a piece of thin cloth or mosquito net over the mouth of the bottle. Study the larvæ for several days, and describe the changes which take place.
3. In what ways does the house-fly transmit the germs of diseases?
4. How can we prevent the house-fly being a danger to health?
5. Why does the house-fly deposit its eggs in decaying matter?

6. Fill in the blanks:
   (a) The fly is a harmless-looking ——, but in reality it is a very —— one.
   (*b*) It may rest on —— in the street, and then straight way —— on some article of food which has been left un ——.
   (c) The house-fly does not —— man or animals; it is a —— insect.
   (*d*) It cannot eat —— food, but has to —— it first.
   (*e*) You would not recognize the —— when they have changed into the pupæ, as both their —— and their —— are different.
   (*f*) The best way to destroy rubbish is to —— it.

LESSON 6

THE VOYAGES OF COLUMBUS—I

[*Note to Teacher.*—Before reading this lesson, revise Lesson 19 in Book II.]

THE FIRST VOYAGE

WE have already read of the great Genoese navigator, who was one of the first to believe in the roundness of the earth, and to whom all the West Indian islands of importance, except Barbados, owe their discovery. On August 3, 1492, after many difficulties in obtaining ships and men, Christopher Columbus set sail from Palos in Spain, in his ship the *Santa Maria,* on his first voyage of discovery, accompanied by Martin Alonzo Pinzon in the *Pinta,* and Vincente Yañez Pinzon in the *Nina*. An accident to the *Pinta's* rudder caused a delay of nearly a month off the Canary Islands; but on the 6th of September the expedition set sail again steering a course for the west.

Henceforward Columbus had more difficulty in keeping his crews in good heart than in navigating his vessels. Frequently the men threatened to mutiny, and matters became serious when the ships entered the mass of floating weed in the Sargasso Sea of which you read in Book III., as the terrified sailors believed that the ships were in imminent danger of running aground. By keeping two logs, however, one secret and accurate, and the other false for the inspection of the men, Columbus succeeded in concealing from them their true position, and so averted the insurrection.

On the 1st of October, by the Admiral's own reckoning, they had crossed 2,100 miles of sea, and still they were surrounded by the waves. The water was full of fish, particularly of flying-fish which skimmed the surface of the waves, and flocks of birds passed overhead, but there was nothing else to interest the voyagers.

A sum of money had been promised to him who first saw land, and all day long the excited men were persuading themselves that this or that cloud was some island, and startling the whole ship with their shouts. Many were the false alarms, and eventually the sailors on the *Santa Maria* rose up in a body and refused to go farther, demanding to return to Spain, or they would select a new captain to take them back. Columbus realized that on this occasion he could not master them as he had done before, but so sure was he that land must be near, that he said very quietly, without betraying the anxiety he felt, "Give me, my men, but three days." The men assented silently and moved away, working and waiting for the third day, when they might turn homewards.

"GIVE ME, MY MEN, BUT THREE DAYS."

(*See page 90.*)

Two whole days went by, and Columbus's hopes fell lower. But on Thursday, the 11th of October, the sailors picked up a branch with fresh red berries on it, which must have been recently broken off. They found, too, some river weed, and a small cane which had been cut by a man's hand. They were all excited by these discoveries, and that night no man went to sleep, while the Admiral himself watched from the high poop of his vessel. During the night a light was seen, and as they watched they saw that it moved a little and sometimes was hidden altogether, as though some person were carrying a torch among trees.

The *Santa Maria.*
(*From a drawing supposed to be by Columbus.*)

At last, in the early hours of the morning the outline of an island was seen looming through the darkness, and as it grew lighter land could unmistakably be seen about six miles away. The men sang and leapt, and even wept, while they praised God who had brought them safely through their perilous voyage.

The New Lands

When the sun rose on 12th October 1492, the sailors saw before them an island several miles long, covered with trees. The sea was calm, the sky without a cloud, and they could distinguish figures coming from the woods and collecting on the shore to gaze at the strange vessels. A boat was lowered, and the Admiral, dressed gorgeously in red, took his seat in it, holding the royal standard of Spain. The brothers Pinzon, his captains, bore two banners embroidered with green crosses and a large "F" and "I" for Ferdinand and Isabella, the King and Queen of Spain.

The natives watched the movements of the Spaniards from a distance in absolute quiet. As soon as Columbus reached dry land, he fell on his knees and kissed the ground, calling out for joy with tears in his eyes. After returning thanks to God, he very solemnly named the island San Salvador, and took possession of it in the name of the King and Queen of Spain. The native name for the island was Guanahani, and we now know it as Watling Island, one of the Bahamas.

The inhabitants soon became friendly, and offered the sailors tame parrots, cotton thread wound in skeins, and cassava bread, in exchange for pieces of broken china, rusty nails, or coloured beads. In the words of Columbus, "They took all, and gave what they had with a good will." Some of them wore little gold rings in their noses, and the sight of this metal raised the hopes of Columbus, giving him visions of returning to his King with valuable treasure. He asked the natives where they found it, and they pointed to the south, and made him understand, partly by signs and partly because he had already managed to learn a few of their words, that a large island lay there in which much of this yellow metal was to be had.

After exploring the island for three days, he again set sail, and the following day reached another island which is now called Rum Kay, but which he named Santa Maria de la Concepcion. He then proceeded to Long and Crooked Islands, where he speaks of having seen tall palm-trees, numerous lizards and parrots, while the sea contained "fish of every hue," and even whales.

Hearing again of the large island to the south where there was an abundance of the precious metal, he concluded it must be Japan, as he, of course, imagined himself to be in the neighbourhood of India. Four days later he reached its north coast, and entered a harbour at the mouth of a deep wide river. This island, which he called Juana (now Cuba), was much larger and more beautiful than any the Spaniards had yet seen. The lofty hills were covered with dense forest, among the flowers of which flitted myriads of hummingbirds. Gorgeously glittering beetles crawled about on the ground, and strange scented trees, in which Columbus fancied he had found the spices of Asia, grew everywhere. Best of all, he believed he had found the pearl oyster itself among the rocks at the river mouth.

After staying some time and sailing along the north coast of Cuba, but finding no trace of gold nor pearls in the oyster shells, he decided to try the other direction, and to make for another island of which the natives continually talked to him.

For some days they were delayed by contrary winds, but on the 6th of December, away to the east, they came upon a great island, which he called Hispaniola from its resemblance to Spain. The mountains were higher than those in Cuba, but the woods did not cover the whole island, large open green spaces being seen. The smoke rising in all directions showed that there were many inhabitants, and Columbus wrote of them: "All have a loving manner and gentle speech. Their houses and villages are pretty, each with a chief who acts as their judge, and who is obeyed by them. All these lords use few words, and have excellent manners. Most of their orders are given by a sign."

So far all had gone well with the adventurers, but on Christmas Day they met with their first great misfortune. Through the carelessness of the seaman on watch the *Santa Maria* drifted towards the shore and struck heavily on a reef, becoming a total wreck. As Alonzo Pinzon had previously sailed off alone, Columbus was now in a great difficulty. The small *Nina* could not hold nearly all the men, and some must be left behind. He determined to build a fort and leave a small colony in it until he returned again from Europe. When the fort was finished he held a great ceremony and named it La Navidad—the Nativity, or Birth of Christ—and fired off a salute with his largest guns.

On the 4th of January the Admiral left Navidad, keeping his course to the east, and afterwards came up with the *Pinta* again. He intended to call at some of the smaller islands before beginning his return voyage across the Atlantic, but on the 16th of January there was such a favourable wind blowing that he determined not to delay. After another perilous journey, in which they again lost sight of the *Pinta,* the little *Nina* eventually reached Spain.

The brave mariner was received with much rejoicing, and marched in a procession to the Royal Palace, where he related his wonderful news to the King and Queen. All Europe resounded with his praises, and his adventure was looked upon in the nature of a miracle. No one knew, however, its true greatness: all thought, not that a vast new continent had been found, but that Columbus had reached some islands off the east coast of India; and because the islands had been found by sailing to the west, they were named the West Indies, and this name, as you know, they keep to this day.

Exercises

1. How many ships took part in the first voyage? Say what happened to each.
2. Why did Columbus think he would find gold in the islands? Was he successful?
3. What was the greatest difficulty which faced Columbus on his outward voyage? How did he overcome it?
4. Trace the first voyage on the chart on page 62. Indicate these islands at which he called in the order named: Watling Island, Rum Kay, Long Island, Crooked Island, Cuba, and Hispaniola.
5. Why was the fort established at Navidad? Why was it so called?
6. Fill in the blanks:
   (*a*) Although Columbus was an ——, he won more glory for —— than any of her own ——. He crossed the —— —— without a guide or ——.
   (*b*) The canoes of the —— held as many as forty ——, and were rowed with short, wide ——.
   (*c*) The mountains were higher in —— than in ——.
   (*d*) One marvellous thing the Spaniards saw was men and women putting rolls of leaves in their ——, lighting ——, and swallowing the smoke. The leaves used by these fire-eaters were named ——.
   (*e*) On the way home they sighted land in the Atlantic. It was one of the —— of the —— which belonged to Portugal.

LESSON 7

PICTURE LESSONS—II

INTERIOR OF A DUTCH HOUSE

WE can learn a great deal from the picture on the next page. It tells us something about the architecture, the costumes, and the customs of the people of Holland of two centuries ago.

It shows us the interior of a living-room, with its raftered ceiling and black-and-white tiled floor. There are windows on the left side, and an old map and a painting on the back wall.

The map reminds us that the Dutch have always been great travellers and explorers; and the picture, that some of the world's greatest artists were Dutchmen. (See pages 75, 95, 168, and 185.)

Four people are in the room—two men sitting at a table, and two women standing. Do you think you could make up a story about those four people? It may help you if we look more closely at them.

The men are gaily dressed in the fashion of the period. Their hanging locks are like those of the Cavaliers of Oliver Cromwell's time. One has on his knee a high-crowned hat with a huge feather in it. They seem to be paying a call on the nearer lady, who has a glass of wine in her hand which she is evidently going to give to some one.

In the original picture there are some details which we can hardly see in this small copy. The farther gentleman has a long clay tobacco-pipe in his hand. It is so like the colour of his coat that it is just visible.

INTERIOR OF A DUTCH HOUSE.
(*Pieter de Hooch, 1629–78.*)

There are some small objects lying on the floor at the front of the picture. They appear to be a broken tobacco-pipe and a piece of paper which has held tobacco. The serving-maid seems to be bringing to the table a brazier with red-hot charcoal in it. The men will light their pipes from it. Why did they not use matches?

We can see the floor through the skirt of the serving-maid. Let me tell you the reason for this. The picture had no maid in it when it was first painted. But as it looked ill-balanced the artist painted the maid, over the painting of the floor, to restore the balance of the composition. The skirt was thinly painted. The solid painting of the floor is now shining through it.

Is this a detailed picture, or has the artist only tried to give a general impression of what is happening?

The colours are very bright and full of contrasts. We say that this is a good "decorative" picture.

LESSON 8

DISPERSAL OF SEEDS

HUMAN beings do not thrive when they live in overcrowded places; similarly, plants do not develop to perfection unless they can obtain the amount of air, sunlight, and food which they need. Nature has therefore provided many means for the wide dispersal of plants, and has adapted them and their seeds accordingly.

Some seeds have special contrivances attached to them for this purpose, whilst the fruits of others are so made as to facilitate the dispersal of the seeds they contain. In this lesson we shall consider the part that both methods play.

Many seeds merely drop to the ground and grow. Some of the seedlings soon outstrip the others and eventually smother them, thus illustrating the old doctrine of "the survival of the fittest." The high woods or tropical forests furnish many good examples of this, as there many sizes of seedlings of large trees may be seen, all competing in the struggle for air, sunlight, and food.

The aim of most plants, however, is to spread their seeds as far as possible from themselves in order to give the seedlings room to develop into strong plants. Sometimes the plants do this of their own accord, but often the seeds are so adapted as to be able to make use of other agencies, the four chief of these being: (1) wind; (2) animals; (3) water; and (4) special plant devices.

Apart from these definite and well-known agencies by which seeds are dispersed there are some others more or less accidental. Nowadays, with the many rapid means of transport over different parts of the globe, seeds of both crop plants and weeds may be carried long distances in packing materials. Seeds originally collected and distributed for garden and farm purposes sometimes become so naturalized in their new home that they eventually grow wild. The sacks which contain the seeds of crop plants may also hold mixed with them the seeds of weeds, which may establish themselves in their new habitat and become pests. You will learn more about this in the lesson on "Weeds." We will now consider separately the four chief methods of dispersal.

1. *Dispersal by Wind*

Seeds capable of being carried by the wind are either very small and light, or they are supplied with appendages which are able to buoy them up in the air sufficiently long for them to be borne considerable distances, in the same manner as the wings of an aeroplane support the weight of its body and engine.

Cedar Capsule and Winged Seed.

Examples of small wind-borne seeds are those of orchids, which are produced in large numbers and blown on to adjoining trees.

The seeds of both mahogany and cedar are provided with tiny wings. The fruit splits lengthwise when it is ripe, and the wing enables the seeds to be carried along and gradually lowered to the ground.

Easter Flower and Winged Fruit.

The Easter Flower* is an instance in which a wing is attached to the fruit, to act as a plane for the wind to carry it along. It will interest you to take either this fruit or the seeds of the

* Securidaca.

mahogany and cedar and throw them into the air to see how they fall.

Seeds of the silk-cotton tree have silky floss attached to them, and it is a familiar sight in the West Indies when the pods burst to see these seeds being borne by the wind for long distances, supported by the floss. The "old man's beard" is another plant whose seeds are provided with silky hairs to enable them to float in the wind.

Wind also plays its part in seed distribution by swaying plants and scattering their ripe seeds in all directions.

2. *Dispersal by Animals*

Some small seeds and fruits are prickly or sticky, and others are provided with little hooks. These are able to fasten themselves on to the coats of animals brushing past them or even on to our clothes. The railway daisy is a well-known plant whose seeds attach themselves to one's clothes by little hooks.

Desmodium, or Sweethearts' Grass.

You know, too, that if you examine your clothes after passing through grass or bush, you will find adhering to them seeds of plants such as desmodium and the sensitive plant and certain prickly grass seeds; the little burr-like seeds of the cousin mahoe may also be among them. The seed of the leadwort, or plumbago, fastens itself by means of sticky glands.

If attached to an animal, these seeds sooner or later fall from its coat to the ground, and under favourable conditions there they will grow. In cleaning your clothes of such seeds you also unwittingly assist in seed dispersal.

Other seeds are contained in attractively coloured edible fruits; after these are devoured by birds or animals the seeds pass through their bodies unharmed, and are often deposited far from the parent plant. Small animals, such as squirrels, when collecting nuts for food, often drop some of them to the ground; bats also eat fruits and drop the seeds; whilst sticky seeds may attach themselves to the beaks of birds, and the bird when cleaning its beak acts as a seed distributor.

3. *Dispersal by Water*

Water plays an important part in the dispersal of seeds and fruits, whether in the form of the sea, or rivers, or flood waters.

The coconut is a common example of distribution by sea. The buoyant fibrous fruit is provided with a waterproof coating which protects the hard-shelled nut, or seed, from injury by the sea water, and the whole fruit is capable of floating in water without suffering any harm. When washed up on a sandy shore coconuts find suitable conditions for germination.

If you examine the high-water mark along some of our beaches, you will see that many seeds and fruits of different kinds have been washed up by the sea, having been brought there from different places around the coast or from other lands. In Trinidad and Tobago, for example, many seeds found on the seashore are known to have come from the region of the Orinoco, the common name for some being "Rocos," a corruption of the name of that mighty river on the Main. Heavy rains, which occasionally flood the land, transport many light seeds considerable distances, and it is a common sight to see quantities of such seeds floating on streams and rivers.

4. *Special Plant Devices*

Some pods when ripe open with explosive force, and scatter their seeds in all directions. Most of you will have noticed during the heat of the day the bursting of the pods of Barbados pride. Other common examples of this method of dispersal are the pods of the sandbox tree, which split into sections, as also do those of the Para rubber tree. These all burst with considerable force, often making quite a loud noise, and discharge their seeds over a wide area.

Sand-box Seed.

The garden balsam is another well-known instance of this device, and it was given its botanical name *Impatiens* because of this explosive or impatient character of the pods.

Thus you see that Nature has provided many ways by which plants may spread themselves, and we human beings often assist in the work without knowing we are doing so.

Exercises

1. Make a collection of various fruits and seeds, and try to decide for yourself by what means they are spread.
2. Why has Nature provided ways for plants to spread their seeds as far as possible?
3. Give examples of seeds which are spread by each of these four methods—wind, animals, water, and special devices.
4. What words in the lesson have a similar meaning to the following?—

congested	from one end to the other
to make easy	something attached
natural abode	sticking to
light	share

5. Fill in the blanks:
   (*a*) The —— or —— of several —— American plants are found on the shores of our —— —— islands.
   (*b*) Many seeds readily —— in the air, as they are —— and light. Other larger ones are —— about in a —— manner when provided with ——.
   (*c*) Among the seeds which stick to our clothing are those of the ——, ——, ——, and ——.
   (*d*) When a —— eats the fruit of the mistletoe the —— stick to —— bill. It then —— its beak by —— it on the bark of the —— on which it has been feeding. The seeds —— and grow there.
6. Why do you think it is better for a plant to shake its seeds out of the top of its seed-box than to drop them out of holes at the bottom?
7. Make drawings of the seeds shown in the sketches. Do the same with any other interesting seeds in your collection.
8. Place a nearly ripe fruit of the sand-box tree or a ripe spike of the castor-oil plant in the sun. Measure, after the explosion, how far the seeds have been dispersed.

LESSON 9

IN THE GOLD AND DIAMOND FIELDS OF GUYANA

ALTHOUGH the industries of the West Indies and the neighbouring countries on the Main are chiefly agricultural or the raising of crops, yet there are also valuable mineral products to be obtained in this part of the world, as we saw when reading of the "Oilfields of Trinidad." The precious metal, gold, which draws men to it like a magnet, and the most valuable of jewels, diamonds, have been found in considerable quantities during recent years in Guyana, the only British colony on the mainland of South America.

We shall see in a later lesson in this book that the legend respecting gold discoveries in that country dates back to the time of Sir Walter Raleigh, who searched there in vain for the fabled city of El Dorado. Apart from the fact that he actually obtained gold in small quantities from the Indians, his prophecies that the precious metal would be found there remained unfulfilled for hundreds of years. It was, however, no doubt the belief in the existence of the Golden City that led to the first systematic attempt to find gold in the colonies which now form Guyana.

In 1720 parties of adventurers went up the Berbice, Essequibo, Mazaruni, and Cuyuni Rivers with this object in view, but they met with scant success. Towards the end of the nineteenth century, however, gold was found and the industry made rapid headway. As soon as it was known that the precious metal really

Gold mining dredger.

existed in the colony in paying quantities, there was the usual rush to the neighbourhood.

The gold and diamond fields, known locally as the gold diggings, are situated far away from the flat inhabited coast lands of Guyana. They extend over a very wide area of the country along the upper reaches of the banks and basins of the Demerara, Berbice, Barima, and Essequibo Rivers and their tributaries. These districts are known as the interior, and the transport thither of men and materials has to be made from the coast lands in open boats up the rivers. This is a difficult and often a dangerous enterprise, as many angry rapids and falls have to be negotiated on the journey. It must be remembered, too, that Guyana is a very extensive country, the Essequibo River itself being over 500 miles long.

Let us take an imaginary journey to the gold-fields from Georgetown, the capital of the colony and the port of call for all incoming vessels. We have a choice of routes up either the Demerara or the Essequibo Rivers, but will decide on the latter.

Boarding the large steam-ferry at the Stellings, or landing-stage, we cross the Demerara River to Vreedenhoop, and then travel by train across the stretch of flat land which lies between this river and its mightier sister the Essequibo, to Parika, a small town at the mouth of the latter river. There we embark on another steamer in which we sail some fifty miles up the giant Essequibo to Bartica, where we leave the comfort of our vessel for the privations of a journey in open boats to our destination far up either the Mazaruni or the Cuyuni branch of the Essequibo. This is necessary, as only small craft can be taken up the rapids and through their whirling eddies. Many lives have been lost in these angry waters and in the falls we shall encounter on our journey.

At last, after much weary toil, we reach our landing-place, and we find ourselves in the gold and diamond fields. Being eager to see how these precious minerals are obtained, we hurry through the district near the river bank, known as the water-side, and journey inland until we come to the scene of operations.

Here is a party of men in their working garments, which merely consist of a short-sleeved shirt and a pair of short pants, just commencing to clear a piece of land beneath which they hope to find gold. See how busy they are wielding their axes and cutlasses to remove the trees and bush; other men are engaged in making tents or logies with some of the branches of the trees. Notice how well fitted they seem to be for this strenuous work; they are all of negro race, and they look strong and capable of great endurance. Their East Indian neighbours are not sufficiently robust to stand the rough life of the gold and diamond fields.

Over there in a cleared space another party of men is making a large excavation in the ground with their pickaxes and shovels. Despite the loneliness of the situation and the dreariness of the forest, the workers are happy in their toil, chanting their spirited ditties and self-composed folk-songs with great gusto, and exchanging humorous banter while they work.

Midday has arrived since we landed, and the men cease operations and gather in groups to partake of the meal which was being prepared by boys while the men were at work. After a short rest they resume their digging, and by sunset a deep pit has been dug. Hark! there is the welcome sound of the conch shell which announces that work for the day is to cease, and the busy toilers, who have well earned their night's repose, return to their tents for the evening meal and sound sleep in their hammocks.

Morning dawns, and we see them hurrying off to work again, and following them to the pit, we watch them digging until at last they see in the soil signs of the object of their search. There is a shout of "Gold! Gold!" They then set up a "tom," which is an open wooden box about 8 feet long, $3\frac{1}{2}$ feet wide, and 15 inches deep, with a wire screen of fine mesh fixed at one end, or they put up a "sluice," which is similar to the "tom," but much bigger.

As they dig the gravel which shows indications of the presence of gold, they throw it into the "tom," and other men puddle it against the screen with a constant stream of water brought in through the opposite end of the box. This action liberates the gold from the gravel, and the fine particles of the metal pass through the screen and are caught in quicksilver, which absorbs them almost as a magnet picks up particles of iron or steel from a heap of rubbish. The quicksilver or mercury is placed in a small box just below the "tom"; at the end of the day the mixture of gold and mercury, called amalgam, is placed on a flat iron dish on a fire and roasted until the mercury is driven off and the gold remains as a dull yellow mass. Any large nuggets are caught against the screen and can be picked out by hand. The largest nugget which has been obtained by this means weighed 333 ounces.

We learn from the workers that the search for diamonds is carried on in the same way and very often in the same areas. Several of the older men among the miners recall for our benefit the story of how, in the year 1887 or thereabouts, when the "clean-up" was taking place at the end of a day's work, some stones of a peculiar lustre attracted the attention of the workers in the "tom." On examination these shining pebbles proved to be diamonds. Later on, when a gold expedition was made to the upper reaches of the Mazaruni River, small diamonds of fair size were discovered. Then after a time, when those who mined for gold found that the auriferous regions, or gold-bearing areas, showed signs of exhaustion, they turned their attention to the search for diamonds.

To-day the forest country in the interior is the scene of much activity on the part of the "pork knockers," or "tributors," as they are called, a class of men who were

Diamond Working.

originally labourers in the fields and who have little if any means, as well as by the capitalists, the traders, the merchants, and the diamond buyers. The industry has now become one of the most important in Guyana.

Exercises

1. Use your West Indian Atlas, and find on the map on page 12 all the rivers mentioned in this lesson. Trace the journey to the gold-fields.
2. During the first thirty years of the industry over £8,000,000 worth of gold was exported from Guyana. What was the average annual value?
3. What are the following: a tom, pork-knoekers, the Stellings, auriferous regions, the interior, amalgam, logies?
4. Explain why the gold-fields are difficult to reach.
5. Describe a day at the gold-fields. Imagine you are a worker there and have found a large nugget in the "tom." Tell the story in your own words.

LESSON 10

A WEST INDIAN PICTURE IN VERSE

Introduction.—It is due to the poet Wordsworth, perhaps in a greater measure than to any other, that we can see and appreciate the beauties that are around us in the countryside. He taught the people of his time what we today regard as an obvious truth—that all the elements of true poetry are to be found in their greatest purity in the lives and characteristics of the poor. In the following verses the poet—T. Redcam—has shown himself a true disciple of Wordsworth.

What a simple, homely subject for such beautiful thoughts!—the peasant women who daily trudge to market with their produce of the soil. Poor, perhaps, but not despised, they and their humble occupations are raised to an exalted plane as, like mothers to their children, they provide sustenance for the dwellers in the city.

The Mothers of the City

What is the noise that shuffles
On the roads that lead to the town,
While the city slumbers deeply,
While the hours lie dumbly down,

When the gas-lamps talk together
As they sentry the empty street,
And the silence barely quivers
To the passing of dead men's feet?

Oh, who are the weary pilgrims
That caravan now on the way?
'Tis the burdened market-women
With their hampered donkeys grey.

Through the dim wan mists of the morning
  They come who have travelled far
On the long white roads that glimmer
  To the light of the Morning Star.

On their feet is the mud of the roadway,
  Their frocks with the dust is soiled,
Big baskets wrinkle their foreheads,
  From afar have their footsteps toiled.

They have dug for the yam and the yampie,
  They have gravelled potato hills,
They have delved the red clay where the spider
  His fangs with his venom fills.

And the hot noon sun has dazed them
  As they wrought on the steep hillside,
And marshalled their rows of scallion
  Or scattered the red peas wide.

To their hoe-beat sprang the echoes
  Where the dark woods round them wept;
And the blows of their wielded cutlass
  Stirred the air where the ages slept.

They rose while the land lay sleeping
  In the silvery moonlight drest,
And their shoulders bowed to the burden
  As they tramped to the mountain crest;

As they trudged again to the valley,
  As they toiled by the swamp land's edge,
Where the frog to the lizard mutters
  In the ways of a rank dark sedge.

And they heard where the road was slipping
  The rattle of landslides go,
And the thud of the ripened mango
  In the far dark fields below.

To cherish her son does a mother
  Give the milk of her life-pulse born;
These come as the city mothers,
  Mud-daubed in the ghost-grey morn,–

To pour for the city hunger
  The milk from the country's breast,
Like a mother that toils and labours
  That her baby may feed and rest.

They come through the mist of morning,
  With the black road mud on their feet;
Some trod where wild hill-streams thunder,
  And some where sea-surges beat.

Through the grey morn came the mothers
  Of the city, travelled far,
By the long white roads that glimmer
  To the light of the Morning Star.

T. REDCAM:
Songs and Ballads of Greater Britain.
(By permission of J. M. Dent and Sons, Ltd.)

EXERCISES

1. Try to compose a few verses on "The Fishers of the Sea", taking these as a model.
2. Find out how many feet each line has, and where the strong beat comes in each foot. (See Book III.)
3. Which two words, usually nouns, are used as verbs in these verses?
4. When did the "city mothers" waken?
5. What does the poet describe them as doing before going to market?
6. What noises did they hear in the stillness of the morning?
7. Give other words with similar meaning for:
   shuffles, dumbly, quivers, wan, delved, venom, wrought, cherish.

THE HAY WAIN.
(John Constable, 1776–1837. National Gallery, London.)

LESSON 11

PICTURE LESSONS—III

The Hay Wain

On page 55 you see one of the most famous of English landscape pictures. It was painted by John Constable of East Bergholt, Suffolk, England.

"Honest John Constable," as he was called by his friends, once wrote to a friend: "For the last two years I have been running after other people's pictures and seeking the truth at second hand. I shall return to Bergholt, where I shall try to get a pure and simple manner of painting the scenes that may attract me. There is little or nothing in the exhibitions to look up to. There is room for a *natural painter.*"

Most of the landscape painters of Constable's time learned to paint by copying the pictures of other men. Constable went direct to Nature for his ideas. He says: "I love every stile, and stump, and lane in our village; as long as I am able to hold a brush, I shall never cease to paint them."

In 1824, when Constable was forty-eight years of age, "The Hay Wain" was exhibited at the Paris Salon, where it immediately attracted the attention of all the French landscape painters and art critics.

Let us now look at the picture itself. We see before us a quiet English scene. A hay wain, or wagon, is crossing a ford. At the left side is a red-tiled mill, behind which is a group of tall trees. Sunlit fields and trees occupy the right side and centre, and in the distance is a rather cloudy and stormy sky.

If we examine the picture more closely we shall see that it is full of light. In nearly every part there is a suggestion of raindrops glittering in the sunlight. It looks as if it had been raining recently—as if a shower had just cleared off.

This effect of clearing up after rain had never been painted before, and Constable was so noted for it that his friends used to tease him about it.

Henry Fuseli, the professor of painting, was a very bad painter but a very good joker. He was once seen to put up his umbrella as he entered a picture exhibition. "What are you doing with your umbrella up?" asked a friend. "Oh," replied Fuseli, "I am going to look at Mr. Constable's pictures."

Constable exhibited over a hundred large landscapes at the Royal Academy during his lifetime, but he left thousands of small sketches which he had painted direct from Nature.

He was in the habit of making numberless studies of clouds and skies with no landscapes beneath them. He would often note the time of day when he painted them. By means of these studies he came to understand Nature in all her moods.

The following note is on the back of one of these sky studies: "Fifth of September 1822. Ten o'clock morning; looking south-east, brisk wind at west. Very bright and fresh, grey clouds running fast over a yellow bed, about half-way in the sky."

All great painters give something of their own which is new to the common stock of art knowledge. Constable taught artists to look with new eyes at the beauties of landscape, and to convey these beauties to their paintings—it they could!

COLUMBUS SENT TO SPAIN IN CHAINS.

LESSON 12

THE VOYAGES OF COLUMBUS—II

The Second Voyage

There was no difficulty in getting ships together for a second voyage. Three large vessels, attended by fourteen smaller ones such as he had used before, lay waiting for Columbus in Cadiz Bay. From all sides men pressed to take part in the expedition; sailors, craftsmen and miners who would be useful in the new colony, monks who were to bring to the Indians the Christian faith, and men of noble birth to act as leaders: all were on fire with desire of glory, of riches, of adventure.

On board were stored not only provisions, but spades and ploughs, grain and vine-slips, seeds of oranges, lemons, and other fruit, and calves, goats, sheep, and fowls for the colony. There were also eight pigs, which multiplied so rapidly that the islands were soon full of them, and about twenty horses for the Spanish cavalry.

Diego Columbus went with his brother, and Bartholomew wrote to say that he would follow them out. The ships touched at the Canary Islands, and then sailed steadily across the Atlantic. Columbus steered to the south of his old course, as he hoped to make new discoveries before reaching Navidad. On Sunday, November 3, 1493, seven weeks after they had set out, a pilot cried: "The reward! Land! I see land!" and directly afterwards six green islands were seen.

They were some of the Leeward Islands, and the ships passed from one to another in search of a good harbour.

The first was Dominica, so called from the fact that it was discovered on a Sunday, Santa Maria La Antigua (now simply Antigua), the Virgin Islands (which from their number reminded the navigator of St. Ursula and the eleven thousand virgins), St. Christopher, now St. Kitts (the shape of which resembled, in the eyes of the discoverer, that saint carrying the Saviour), Nevis with its rock-cone covered with a cloud like snow (in Spanish, Nieve), and Marie Galante.

At length the Spaniards landed in Guadaloupe, and pressed inland till they came to a village, finding there sure signs that the natives were cannibals. After a day or two had passed, during which some of his men wandered through the woods without seeing the inhabitants, who had fled, Columbus, fearing that the colonists he had left in Navidad might be running short of provisions, determined not to delay longer among the islands, but to sail to the north-west for Haiti. He reached the eastern point of the island and passed slowly along the north coast, looking out for signs of his old crew. Before reaching the fort he had to cross the mouth of the Golden River. There some of his men who had gone ashore made a horrible discovery. Four corpses bound with grass-ropes were lying in the sun. One had a beard, and they knew him to be a Spaniard, for all the Indians had smooth chins.

A great fear fell upon the expedition, and they moved on in dread of disaster. At night they reached Navidad and found all quiet and dark. Guns were fired, but there was no answering report from the shore. In a few hours a party of Indians in a canoe hailed the vessels. They brought two masks of gold as a present to Columbus from their chief Guacanagari, who, they said, was wounded. Slowly and unwillingly they gave news of the Spaniards he had left behind; some had died of sickness and others had been killed in quarrels which arose among themselves for gold. They also said that two Indian princes from the south had attacked the white men and that the fort had been destroyed.

On the next day a boat's crew landed, and found the stockade broken, the fort level with the ground, and eleven graves, not long made, but already covered with grass. Not a Spaniard could they find to tell the true tale of the disaster.

They now set about choosing a site for the new city to be called Isabella, as the animals could no longer be kept on board, the seeds should be sown, and the men were impatient at being cooped up in the ships. Some fifty miles to the east of Navidad they found a good harbour, and there built their home. But, alas! no sooner had they begun to settle down than fever broke out. Columbus fancied that the sickness was caused by the lack of fresh food, so he determined to dispatch some of the vessels to Spain for provisions, particularly calves and sheep; but he must send in them the promised cargo of gold for the King, and hitherto he had not had time to seek for it.

The little fleet carried a long letter written by the Admiral to the King and Queen. This letter may be seen to-day with the comments of their Majesties in the margin, in which they say they would be glad to see a sample of this often-promised gold.

The rest of this second visit to Hispaniola was a period of trials for Columbus—sickness, rebellion, and disappointment at the failure to find gold; and in April

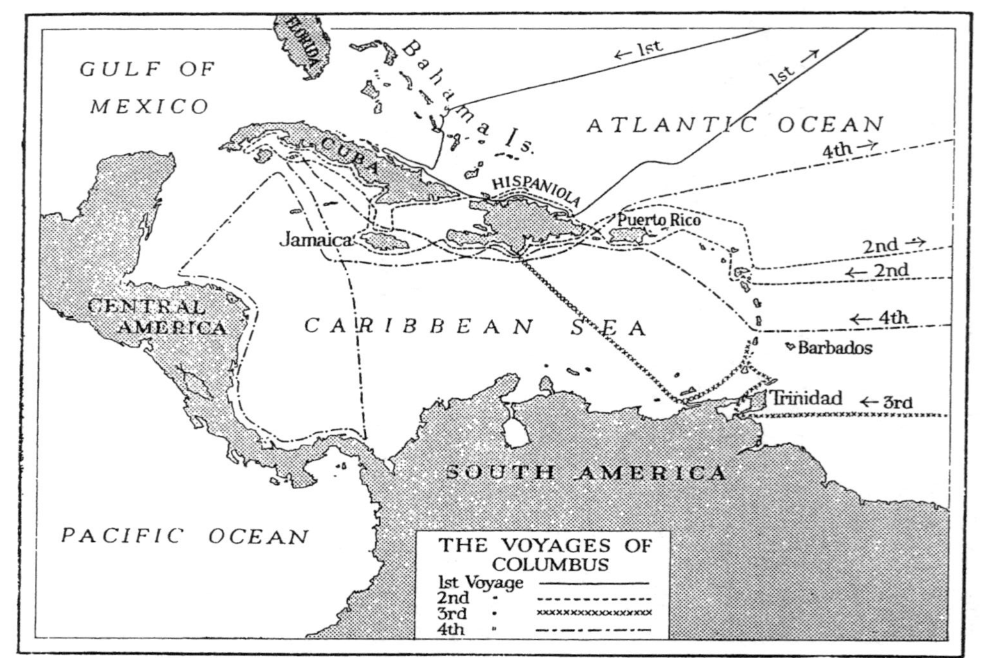
GULF OF MEXICO
FLORIDA
Bahama Is.
← 1st
1st →
ATLANTIC OCEAN
4th →
CUBA
HISPANIOLA
Puerto Rico
Jamaica
2nd →
← 2nd
← 4th
CENTRAL AMERICA
CARIBBEAN SEA
Barbados
Trinidad
← 3rd
SOUTH AMERICA
PACIFIC OCEAN
THE VOYAGES OF COLUMBUS
1st Voyage
2nd "
3rd "
4th "

he left his brother in command of the settlement while he explored the southern coast of Cuba. The natives he met there were full of goodwill, bringing many gifts, and when asked if they had gold, smiled and pointed to the south. The Admiral determined to follow their direction, and after two days reached the island of Jamaica, which he called Xaymaca, where he anchored in St. Ann's Bay.

On the voyage back to Isabella, Columbus became very ill. Various events had happened in the island during his absence; the settlers had rebelled, and new storeships had arrived from Spain and had taken back with them many of the discontented men. When they reached Spain they gave a dismal tale of the new colony, and turned public opinion strongly against Columbus, who met with a very cold reception when he arrived some time afterwards.

The Third Voyage

Queen Isabella had always been the staunch friend of Columbus, and even though it was now generally believed there was but little gold in the islands, she gave orders that eight ships should be provided, furnished with all that he required for another voyage. This time, however, there was no rush of volunteers to embark, and he was forced to take as his crew prisoners who had served part of their sentence and other base men. Two vessels were sent on to Hispaniola with provisions for the colony, and Columbus sailed with the remaining six in May 1498.

He soon gave orders to three more to steer direct to Hispaniola, while with the other three he turned south.

He had come to believe that he would find the mainland more easily, and escape the host of islands, if he kept nearer to the Equator. After touching at the Canary Islands and the Cape Verde Islands, he soon reached the "Doldrums," the region of calms near the Equator. Day after day the ships lay idle on the water, while the sun's hot rays poured upon the decks, and the ocean currents bore them but slowly towards the west. Presently a breeze sprang up, and on the 31st of July a look-out on the mast-head sighted three peaks (now known as the "Three Sisters") on an island. Columbus considered this a happy sign, as he had vowed a short time before to dedicate the first land sighted to the Holy Trinity; so Trinidad the land was named.

Passing along the south coast of the island, he saw land in the distance which he took for another island. But this was really his first glimpse of the mainland of America, the land being the peninsula on the north coast of what is now Venezuela. After endeavouring to find a passage to the west, he finally braved the rushing waters of the Dragon's Mouth, visiting Tobago, Grenada, and St. Vincent on his way to Hispaniola, where more trouble awaited him. Tales of disaster greeted him on every Side; lands unbilled, crops ungathered, mines unworked, and the country plundered by Spaniards and natives in turn.

News of the disturbances eventually reached Spain, and an outcry arose against the once popular Columbus. None of the promised gold had come, but only requests for more provisions, tools, and ships. Discontented sailors declared that he wished to make himself King of Haiti instead of sending its wealth to Spain. The King decided to send out an officer of high rank with power to do anything he thought necessary for the good of the island. One of his first acts was to put the old navigator in chains and send him home to Spain.

As soon as the ships arrived the sovereigns heard of the treatment their great servant had received and they were very indignant. They ordered that he should be set free at once, and he came before the King and Queen, a grey-haired, bent old man, with the story of his misfortunes and sufferings written on his wrinkled face. They talked with him of all his labours, and promised to recall Bobadilla, the officer who had ill-treated him.

The Fourth Voyage

Columbus, who could never be idle, began to dream of a new voyage, which would bring still more glory to Spain. More ships were given to him, and on May 9, 1502, he sailed from Cadiz on his fourth and final voyage. Touching as usual at the Canaries, he took a westerly course, and arrived at St. Lucia, which he sighted on St. Lucy's Day; passing Martinique, he presently put into Puerto Rico, and although he had been expressly ordered not to call at the settlement at Hispaniola, he did so owing to the unseaworthy state of one of his ships. The Governor forbade him to land, and after repairing his vessels he decided to sail for the Gulf of Paria in another attempt to find a passage to the west.

On the 15th of August the coast of Belize was reached, but he was too ill to land and set his foot on the mainland of the continent. His brother Bartholomew took his place and had Mass said on the beach. Cruising slowly eastward in very wild weather, they at last rounded a cape which he named Gracios a Dios, a name it still hears.

Thence they headed south, coasting down the shores of Nicaragua and Costa Rica, and along the northern shore of the narrow isthmus of Panama into the Gulf of Darien. As the coast from this point to Paria had been explored in the meantime by other adventurers, there was no use in sailing farther, and another of his hopes, that of finding a passage to India through this barrier of land, had failed him. His ships were battered and worn, and the return from the most disappointing of his voyages was commenced.

You can read in a little book called *The Story of Columbus* the full story of their journey to Cuba, when they discovered the Cayman Islands, naming them Las Tortugas from the abundance of turtle found there, on to Jamaica and Hispaniola, and so back to Spain for the last time, as well as many other interesting facts about this great man.

Exercises

1. Did Columbus discover the island (or colony) in which you live? If so, on which of his voyages?
2. On a very old map of the world, drawn by an Italian in 1506, we find islands described in Latin as those "which Master Christopher Columbus discovered at the instance of the most serene King of Spain." One important British island does not appear thereon. Which is it? Why is it not shown?
3. Why were the following islands so named?—

   Hispaniola, Dominica, The Virgin Islands, St. Christopher (St. Kitts), Trinidad, St. Lucia, and Las Tortugas (Cayman Islands).

4. *Nevado* is a Spanish word which means *covered with snow.* Why did Columbus name one of the islands *Nevis?*
5. Which do you consider was the most successful of the voyages? Which the least successful? Give reasons in each case.
6. Tell the story of the first colony established by the Spaniards in the West Indies.
7. Trace the voyages carefully on the chart on page 62. With the aid of a good map of the West Indies, such as that on page 6 of the West Indian Atlas, name all the islands shown on the chart.
8. Why is no homeward route shown on the chart for the third voyage? How did Columbus reach Spain on that occasion?

LESSON 13

AIR

THE earth on which we live is surrounded by a great collection of gases, known as the air or the atmosphere, which forms an outer covering or shell many miles in thickness or depth. The study of the atmosphere is of great interest, but in this lesson we can only consider air so far as it affects health.

Air is invisible, and we are only aware of it when portions of it move and produce breezes or winds, or when we ourselves move fast and feel the air pressing against us. It has no taste, nor can we smell it when it is pure. Its existence, however, is of vital importance, for if there were no air, animals and plants could not live, and the earth would be a cold and silent world.

For a long time it was thought that air was a single substance, but the discovery was made many years ago that it is a mixture of several gases. These gases have no common names, and you must therefore learn their scientific ones; they are *oxygen, nitrogen,* and *carbon dioxide,* and they occur in certain definite proportions.

In any 100 volumes of air collected in the open, there are about 20·93 volumes of oxygen, 79·04 volumes of nitrogen, and ·03 of carbon dioxide. There are also present traces of other gases, water in the form of vapour, and exceedingly minute solid particles or dust. You can see these small particles in a sunbeam.

Oxygen is the most important constituent of air. We saw in the lesson on "The Blood" that the red corpuscles carry this gas to all parts of the body, giving up to each part the supply which is necessary to keep it alive. Oxygen therefore is the element that sustains animal life; it is also necessary for all forms of combustion or burning. The following two simple experiments will illustrate these points:

(*a*) *Try* holding your breath. After about three-quarters of a minute you will be very uncomfortable and feel that you *must* breathe. This is due to the blood calling for oxygen, which, as you know, is taken up from the air in the air cells of the lungs by the red corpuscles of the blood and carried to the tissues of the body.

(*b*) Place a lighted match or thin slip of wood in a bottle with a wide mouth. The match will continue to burn for a short time only, and the flame will die out as soon as the oxygen of the air in the bottle is used up. Withdraw the match before this takes place and the flame will brighten up again.

Nitrogen takes no part in sustaining animal life. It does neither harm nor good, as we breathe it in and breathe it out again unchanged. It serves, however, to dilute the oxygen, just as water is used to weaken or dilute strong medicines. In this way it prevents us breathing pure oxygen, which is too strong to breathe continuously.

Carbon Dioxide, though occurring in so small a quantity, is an important constituent of air. It is constantly being formed in the tissues of our bodies, and is one of the waste products which must be regularly removed. This duty is performed by the red blood corpuscles of the blood, which, after giving up oxygen to the tissues, take in the carbon dioxide and carry it to the lungs, where it passes through the thin membranes of the air cells and is breathed out.

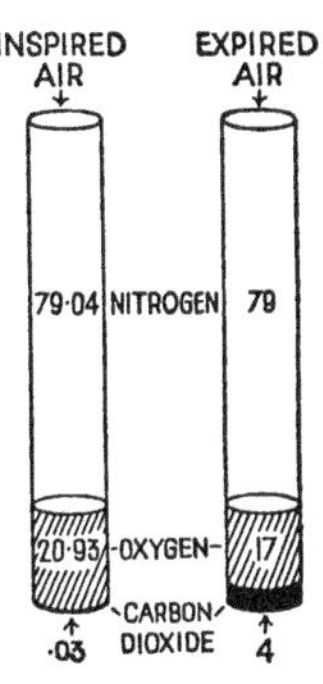

As a result of this interchange there is a remarkable difference between the air we breathe in (inspired air) and the air we breathe out (expired air), as shown in the following table:

	Oxygen.	Nitrogen.	Carbon Dioxide.	
Inspired air.	20·93	79·04	·03	per 100 volumes.
Expired air.	17·0	79·0	4·0	per 100 volumes.

Carbon dioxide is also formed whenever burning or combustion takes place, and it might appear strange that when such large amounts are produced, it does not collect in such quantities as to cause harm. This does not happen for the reason that the green leaves of plants have the wonderful property of breaking up this gas, setting free the oxygen, and absorbing the carbon. You will learn more of this in the lessons on "The Living Plant" in Book V.

It will now be evident that, unless our lungs are supplied with good fresh air, our bodies will not receive their proper and sufficient supplies of oxygen, and will suffer in health. That we do suffer under such circumstances is proved by the fact that persons who live or work in badly ventilated houses—that is, houses not provided with sufficient windows or other openings to admit fresh air—are subject to headaches, have poor appetites, become listless, are tired after slight exertion, and are liable to infection from common colds, tuberculosis, and other diseases. People who live much in the open air, however, have healthy appetites blood of a higher quality, and a better muscular tone.

When people breathe air containing a large quantity of carbon dioxide they soon feel unwell, and if the amount becomes too great it is very dangerous to health. We must therefore be very careful, particularly at nights or when we shut out rain, to see that plenty of fresh air can get in to replace the bad air overcharged with the poisonous carbon dioxide which we have breathed from our lungs.

Ventilation is required in all rooms to allow the movement of air which is so necessary to keep it pure. An adult needs at least 3,000 cubic feet of fresh air each hour, and a child about 2,250 cubic feet. Our homes, therefore, should be properly supplied with windows, jalousies, and doors which will admit this amount of fresh air without causing draughts.

There is a very common custom in the West Indies of closing up every crack or crevice that lets in air, and another foolish habit of covering up the head, which makes you breathe in again a large amount of the air you have breathed out. This is due to a common belief that night air is bad. There is no truth in this belief. People originally covered up their heads to avoid mosquitoes, and so prevent fever, but after your previous lessons you should know that it is not the night air which "gives fever" but the mosquitoes, which are active and bite in the night. You can ward off the attacks of these insects by nets, but you should not shut out the fresh air which is necessary to supply your bodies with oxygen.

Fresh air is never harmful if our bodies are sufficiently protected by clothes. You can avoid chill by seeing that you are not lying in draughts and by using warm coverings; you need then have no fear of letting in the night air. The only bad air is the air of ill-ventilated rooms, and the air which contains poisonous gases or dust particles given off by decaying matter or other harmful substances.

You have doubtless experienced a pleasant and stimulating feeling when you step out of a full or crowded room into the open air. This effect is produced not only by the fresh air inhaled, but also by the bath of air which our bodies get when we move out from a close room to the open air.

The close or stuffy feeling in the room was largely due to the air immediately about our bodies not being changed rapidly enough. This still air forms an envelope or blanket about our bodies, interferes with the passage of heat and moisture, and produces discomfort which in extreme cases may amount to a feeling of suffocation. Remember, then, that *fresh air is Nature's great tonic*; it stimulates the appetite, improves digestion, increases our resistance to disease, and gives us that feeling of fitness and well-being which enables us to enjoy and make the best use of our lives.

Exercises

1. Of what gases is the air composed? Which is present in the greatest quantity? Which is of the greatest use? Which is the most harmful?
2. In what ways does the work of the red blood corpuscles affect the composition of the air we breathe?
3. How is the air kept pure?
4. What do you mean by *ventilation*? How are West Indian houses ventilated? Jalousies are practically unknown in colder countries, yet they are very common here. Why is this?
5. What common customs in the West Indies are very foolish? Explain why they are foolish and why they may do harm rather than good.
6. Fill in the blanks:
   (*a*) The —— covers the earth all over, and extends —— up. It gets thinner and thinner the —— one goes; it also becomes —— and —— in higher altitudes, as you know from the fact that even in the tropics snow will —— on the tops of very high ——.
   (*b*) We human —— live at the —— of a great ocean of ——, just as fishes live in a great —— of water. If you remove the —— from water they die, and in a similar way if —— beings are taken away from air they ——; if poison is —— with the water the fishes will be ——, and in like —— if the —— is poisoned it will kill men.

LESSON 14

WHAT CAN A LITTLE CHAP DO?

Here is a fine poem for boys. The writer, John Oxenham, has given us much food for thought and helpful advice in many of his verses, but never more successfully than in this fine but simple outline of the ideal boyhood. All boys (and girls too) will find it a guiding star.

WHAT can a little chap do
For his country and for you?
What can a little chap do?

He can play a straight game all through;
That's one good thing he can do.

He can fight like a Knight
For the Truth and the Right;
That's another good thing he can do.

He can shun all that's mean,
He can keep himself clean,
Both without and within;
That's a very fine thing he can do.

His soul he can brace
Against anything base,
And the trace will be seen
All his life in his face;
That's an excellent thing he can do.

He can look to the Light,
He can keep his thought white,
He can fight the great fight,
He can do with his might
What is good in God's sight;
These are truly great things he can do.

Though his years be but few,
If he keeps himself true
He can march in the queue
Of the Good and the Great,
Who battled with fate
And won through;
   That's a wonderful thing he can do.

And in each little thing
He can follow the King;
Yes, in each smallest thing
He can follow the King,
He can follow the Christ the King.

JOHN OXENHAM.
(*By permission of the Author.*)

EXERCISES

1. What do you notice about the verses which end with the line in italics? What device does the poet employ to emphasize each point slightly more than the previous one?
2. How does he avoid monotony in the repetition of the line in italics?
3. With this poem as a model, try to compose a series of verses on "How should a little girl play?"
4. What is meant by "a straight game," "anything base," "the queue," "won through," and "Though his years be but few"?

LESSON 15

PICTURE LESSONS— IV

THE CONCERT

THIS is a very simple scene, containing only three figures. Its title, "The Concert," may seem to us too grand,

THE CONCERT.
(*Gerhard Terborch. 1617–81.*)

because we think of a concert as being given by a great many musicians before a very large number of people. Its original meaning had nothing to do with large numbers, but only meant "concerted" music, or music made by two or more people.

In the picture the seated lady is singing a song, at the same time keeping time to the music with her right hand. The standing lady is accompanying her on a guitar.

Do you think the ladies are related to each other? Sisters, perhaps, or even twins? Sometimes artists paint the same person in different positions in the same picture, and it seems not unlikely that this has been done in this painting.

Why has the artist painted the boy? Can you tell what he is carrying? Can you imagine what the picture would have looked like without the boy?

There would have been only two figures, and the sitting lady, who is now in the centre of the group, would have been at the right side of the picture. As she is now, in the centre of the picture with a figure on each side, she is in the most important position.

We can see that this has been the artist's intention, as he has dressed her in white, while the two other figures are in duller colours. The bright scarlet of her chair also helps to attract the eye. Artists have different ways of directing our attention to the principal figure in a picture. In this case it has been done by light and bright colours.

Have you noticed that the background behind the figures is dull in colour, and has no definite shapes of furniture, doors, or pictures? This has been done purposely, so that the eye is not drawn away from the group of figures, and especially from the central one.

Can you see the fingerboard of the guitar or the details of the standing lady's dress clearly? The clever artist has painted such things indistinctly, so that our eyes may rest with pleasure on what he thinks are the more interesting parts of the picture.

We may thus enjoy the wonderful sheen on the central lady's dress, the delicate drawing, colouring, and modelling of all the faces and hands, as well as the pattern of the table-cover.

By noticing such things we begin to understand not only the "story" which the artist tries to tell us, but also what means he has employed to make his picture pleasing to us.

What a great deal of thought this artist has put into his picture, which seems so easy and natural—after it is painted! The general colour effect is very pleasing and harmonious. This is because it has both bright and dull colours in it.

Like the picture on page 38, it is a good "decorative" painting. Its subject is not very important or exciting, but the general effect of it is pleasing, and it brightens up any wall on which it is hung, and especially a rather dark corner.

LESSON 16

LONDON

LONDON is the capital of the United Kingdom and of the British Commonwealth. It is the 15th largest and 5th wealthiest city in the world. It spreads over a space of 671.0 square miles and in this area live an estimated 9,787,426 people. The city stretches for miles along

WINDSOR CASTLE AND THE THAMES.

both banks of the river Thames, which, though a small river as compared with many others, is one of the most famous waterways in the world. It was the chief market for many of the products of other lands, such as tea, coffee, cocoa, spices, and furs. London is a centre of banking and financial business, which counts for much in the affairs of nations. In the busiest part of the City we see the Bank of England. In the street near at hand are the offices of dozens of other banks, smaller, but doing a large and far-reaching business. The money transactions carried on here day by day affect the whole world. The picture on page 83 shows you what the front of the Bank looks like.

The central part of London is called the "City of London." This portion, little more than a square mile in extent, has around 7,375 residents; but over 300,000 commute in daily. Every morning the streets swarm with thousands of hurrying men and women, brought near the scene of their work by trains, underground "tube" railways, taxis and buses; and every evening this human flood ebbs again through the same channels. It is more a "city" of business offices, not of homes.

In London there are many famous buildings which every stranger visits. To the east of the City, on a height overlooking the river, is the Tower, the oldest building in London, founded by Julius Caesar before the birth of Christ, and rebuilt by William the Conqueror and his sons a thousand years afterwards. Once the scene of many a cruel imprisonment and execution, it is now an interesting museum of armour and weapons, a barracks, and a military storehouse. The crown of England and other state jewels are kept in the Tower for all to see.

Some two miles westward, and beyond the limits of the City, stands the world-renowned Westminster Abbey, grey with its thousand birthdays. Here the

London—The River Thames and the Tower Bridge.

kings and queens of England have been crowned since the time of Edward the Confessor, who built it. William the Conqueror was crowned King of England here on Christmas Day, 1066; and here on 2nd June 1953 our Queen Elizabeth was crowned "Queen of Great Britain and Northern Ireland and of her other Realms and Territories, Head of the Commonwealth." Eighteen kings and queens lie buried within its walls, and many more notable figures in history. In the Poets' Corner we see the tombs of those whose names are familiar wherever the English language is spoken—Chaucer, Spenser, Macaulay, Dickens, Tennyson.

Just over the way stands the noble pile of buildings where the British Parliament holds its sessions. Close at hand are the many Government offices, where the army, navy, and other departments are managed and where not only British affairs, but those of the Commonwealth, are carried on.

London—The Tower.

In the centre of the City stands a huge building, whose dome we have noticed rising high into the haze. This is St. Paul's Cathedral, which has well been called the monarch of English churches. In its crypt are the tombs of Nelson, Wellington, and others whose names are written in history. The tall column we have noticed nearer the abbey, rising in the noble space of Trafalgar Square, is a monument to Nelson.

Facing it is the long pillared front of a building well worthy of more visits than one—the National Gallery, where we should find the originals of the pictures on pages 55, 95, and 168 of this book.

A little to the north is a huge square building, which we must not pass by. It is the British Museum. Here is the 2nd largest library in the world. A copy of every book printed in the United Kingdom must be placed upon its shelves, and many others of value are also added year by year. They are carefully guarded, but may be freely used by any who wish to consult them. Old books are here as well as new. There are beautiful volumes written by hand on parchment before printing was invented, and many curious ancient documents from Egypt and other Eastern lands. There are rooms which contain priceless examples of art and industry from Egypt and Turkey and from Greece and Rome, among which we could spend many days.

The streets of London seem strange to us at first. They wind about and cross one another in all directions. There are tens of thousands of them, and it is likely that no Londoner has seen them all. Some are wide and noble, some narrow and mean, but in the central area they all seem too narrow for the tide of traffic which surges through them.

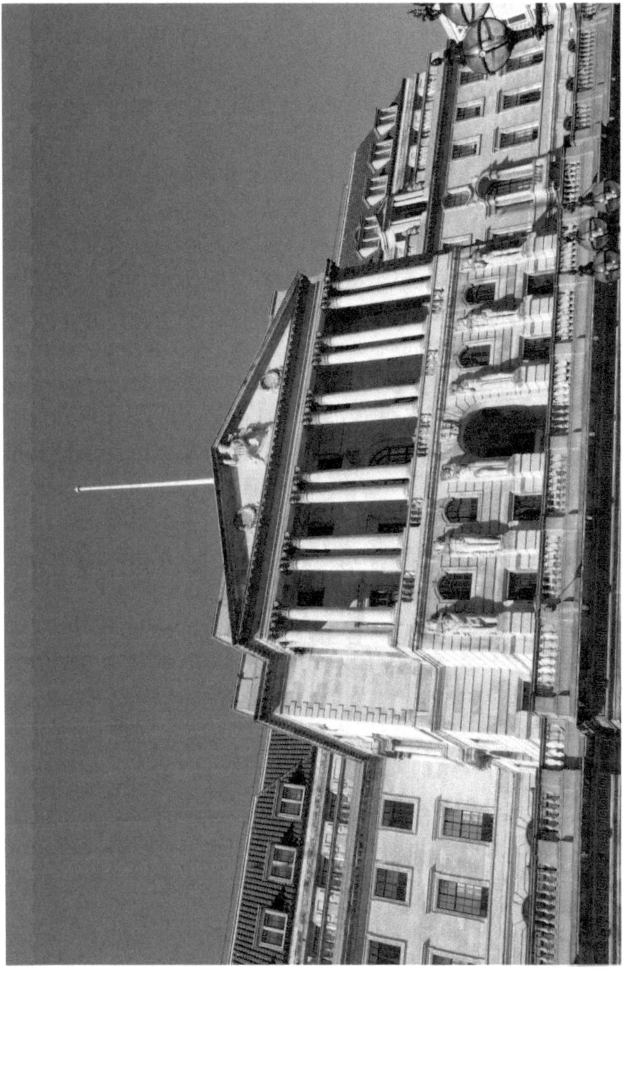

IN THE "CITY" OF LONDON—THE BANK OF ENGLAND.

In some places, there are underground passages, by which one can cross the busiest street without delay or danger.

But London is not all streets. It is well supplied with parks and open spaces, and in many of these we can sit under the trees by the side of beautiful little lakes or ponds and forget that we are in the heart of a great city. A few miles up the Thames we come to Kew Gardens, Richmond Park, and Hampton Court, where there is some of the most beautiful woodland scenery to be seen.

In London itself there are three royal palaces to see, one of which, Buckingham Palace, is shown on page 85, and we may also enjoy a visit to Windsor Castle, farther up the Thames. It stands on a hill on the north bank, and from the top of the Round Tower we have a charming view of English scenery. The oldest parts of the castle were built by William the Conqueror, but it has been much altered and enlarged, and is now a vast and stately pile. In St. George's Chapel, a beautiful building standing within the castle grounds, ten English kings lie buried. It is the long building to the right in the picture on page 78.

Exercises

1. What is the United Kingdom? Make a list of as many countries as you can which are parts of the British Commonwealth. (You can include all our islands under one name—"The British West Indies.")
2. How many people are there in the largest town in your colony? How many in the colony itself? How many times greater is the population of London than that of (*a*) your largest town, (*b*) your colony?

BUCKINGHAM PALACE (THE HOME OF OUR QUEEN) AND QUEEN VICTORIA MEMORIAL.

3. Make a list of the interesting buildings mentioned in this lesson. Say for what each one is famous.
4. Mention some great writers who are buried in Westminster Abbey.
5. Why should every West Indian know something of London? If you had the opportunity to go there what would you most desire to see? Give reasons.
6. Where does the Queen live when she is in London? What other homes has she?
7. Fill in the blanks:
   (*a*) The Queen's crown can be —— in a glass case in the —— of London. An interesting old custom is performed every —— when this historical —— is locked up.
   (*b*) The ships, —— and leaving the Thames, —— cargoes either to be —— or sold, so London could not do without its river.
   (*c*) The place where merchants, bankers, and brokers of a —— meet to —— their business, whether connected with money, corn, coal, provisions, or shipping, is known as an ——. The oldest of these is known as the Royal ——, and it is close to the —— —— —— on page 83.
   (*d*) The building where our money is coined is known as the ——. It is guarded —— and —— by soldiers from the Tower in the neighbourhood.

LESSON 17

THE ISLAND OF GOLD

I

ONE of the finest tales of treasure-hunting ever told is *Monte Cristo,* which was written by the great French writer Alexandre Dumas. When you are older I hope you will read the book as the author wrote it. Perhaps it is in your school library. Here I can only give you an outline of the story.

About a mile outside the harbour of Marseilles there is a rocky islet, on which stands a gloomy prison where men accused of crimes against the State used to be confined. Edmond Dantès, the hero of this story, was a State prisoner who spent a long and weary imprisonment on this island.

He was a young sailor, whose ship had called at the island of Elba, where the Emperor Napoleon was then living. The emperor had been banished to this island, and another ruler had been chosen to take his place. All Frenchmen who held any sort of communication with the exiled emperor were considered to be traitors.

Edmond had been asked to carry a letter from Napoleon to some of his friends in France, and had agreed to do so. He knew nothing of what the letter contained, and was quite unaware that he was doing wrong. He had enemies, however, and they managed to get him thrown into prison on a charge of treason.

He had been many years in prison when one day he heard a noise of scratching on the wall of his cell. It came from a very clever old abbé or priest, who was imprisoned in the next cell, and was trying to loosen some of the stones in the wall so that he might escape.

Edmond was eager to help his fellow-prisoner. He managed to make a tool out of the handle of a saucepan, and with it he worked on his side of the wall. After many months a secret hole was made in the wall, and Edmond and the abbé were able to talk together and to pass from the one cell to the other.

The abbé took a great fancy to Edmond, and became his teacher. At last he felt himself dying, and then he told Edmond that a vast treasure was buried in a grotto on the little uninhabited island of Monte Cristo. After giving his friend full instructions how to find the grotto and the place in it where the treasure was concealed, the abbé died—to Edmond's great grief.

The dead body of the abbé was tied in a sack ready for burial in the sea. After the jailers had left the abbé's cell Edmond entered it by the hole in the wall, and, taking the dead body out of the sack, carried it into his own cell, and placed it on his own bed. Then he crept back into the abbé's cell, and got inside the sack, which he tied up from the inside. He had the abbé's knife with him, but nothing else.

Late that evening the jailers came to take away the dead body. They tied something heavy to the foot of the sack, and, lifting it on to a bier, carried it up to the edge of the cliff overhanging the sea.

"Now then, are you ready?" said one of them.

"One—two—three!"

Edmond felt himself hurled through space, and falling, falling, like a wounded bird. Then there was a terrific noise in his ears, and he felt the cold sea water whirling about him. He had been thrown into the sea with a thirty-six-pound shot tied to the sack to make it sink.

He held his breath, and, rapidly slitting up the sack with his knife, freed himself. He was an excellent swimmer, and he now struck out boldly for the open sea. In the darkness of night he was not seen by the sentinels of the prison.

He meant to swim to a rock that he knew of, not far away; but in the darkness he did not know the

"EDMOND FELT HIMSELF HURLED THROUGH SPACE."

(*See page 88.*)

direction in which it lay. Just then a flash from a lighthouse lit up the waters, and this enabled him to see the rock. He swam steadily towards it, floating on his back from time to time to rest.

The sky grew darker than ever, and an enormous cloud, blacker than the rest, seemed to descend upon him; at the same time he felt a sharp pain in his knee. At first he thought that he had been shot, although he had not heard the report of a gun. He put out his hand, and felt something hard; then he put down his foot, and touched LAND.

He was only twenty yards away from the rock. He walked ashore, and then with a prayer of thankfulness lay down on the hard rocks and slept. He slept soundly in spite of the roaring of the sea and the steady drip of the rain, which now began to fall heavily.

II

A storm raged during the night, but Edmond slept on. He awoke early in the morning, and as he stood looking towards the sunrise he saw a little vessel sailing out of Marseilles. If it continued on the same course it would be sure to pass very near to his rock. If he could but reach it he would be safe.

He descended from the rock, plunged into the water, and swam towards the vessel. Soon he perceived that the ship was only half a mile away, and taking off his cap, he waved it above his head, and uttered one of those long, wailing cries such as sailors in distress are accustomed to give.

The sailors on board the vessel both saw and heard him, and a boat was launched. Before it could reach him, however, a sudden stiffness overcame him; he gave a despairing cry, and the water closed over his head. He seemed to feel some one seizing him by the hair, but that was all.

When he opened his eyes again, he was on the deck of the ship, and far from his prison. He told his rescuers that he was the sole survivor of a ship that had been wrecked on the previous night. They were short-handed, and as Edmond was a capital sailor, they were glad to let him join them. Soon he discovered that he had joined a band of smugglers.

Edmond had many adventures with the smugglers but he never forgot the treasure on the island of Monte Cristo. All his thoughts were devoted to plans for landing on the island and seizing the treasure.

His chance came at last. The smugglers wished to "run" a cargo of Turkey carpets, silks, and cashmeres, but could not do so because the coastguards were on the watch. They therefore decided to land their cargo on the uninhabited island of Monte Cristo and leave it there until the coast was clear.

The ship sailed for the island and anchored in the bay. When the cargo was landed, Edmond took a gun, a powder-flask, and a pick, and with a friend set off to explore the island. He could not, however, search for the treasure, because his friend was with him.

When he returned to the shore he pretended to slip, and with a cry fell to the ground, where he appeared to lie unconscious. His companions rushed to his assistance; but when he came to he complained of great pain, and begged his friends to leave him on the island and pick him up on the return voyage. As the captain was much pressed for time, he agreed to do so.

As soon as the ship disappeared Edmond sprang up, and, taking his gun in his hand, followed the directions of the abbé until he reached a rock which blocked his path. He examined it carefully, but soon he perceived that it was far too big and too heavy for him to move. Then a thought struck him. Why not blow it up with the gunpowder in his flask?

This he did, and when the noise of the explosion died away he found behind the rock, which had been blown into fragments, a square stone with an iron ring attached to it. With the thick branch of an olive tree he raised the stone, and saw beneath it a rough staircase.

Slowly he descended this staircase, and found himself in a grotto. The floor was of fine white sand, and the walls were of glittering granite. There was no sign of any treasure. He took his pick and sounded the walls. The echo on one side assured him that there was a grotto beyond the one in which he was standing.

Lifting his pick, he struck a tremendous blow at the wall, and discovered to his surprise that it was composed not of granite, but of a kind of glaze which had been spread over bricks. Soon Edmond had made a hole big enough to admit him into the second grotto.

He now began to dig in the left-hand corner, as the abbé had instructed him. Suddenly his pick touched something hard. He lighted a pine branch, and, sticking the torch in the ground, began to dig again. Hurrah! He saw before him an oak chest bound with iron clasps. He wrenched off the clasps, and the chest burst open, disclosing gold and silver coins, diamonds, rubies, and pearls—such wealth as he had never even dreamed of!

And here I must end the story. I cannot stay to tell you how Edmond removed the treasure to the mainland, how he became the richest man in all the world, and how he spent his money. You will find the whole story fully told in the fascinating pages of Alexandre Dumas.

Exercises

1. Explain the difference between "bier" and "beer." Make a list of other words you know which are pronounced alike but are spelt differently and have different meanings.
2. What do you know of the Emperor Napoleon? In which lesson did you read of him? What events were happening in the West Indies during his time?
3. Use your atlas to make a sketch-map of France, and show the position of Marseilles. Can you mark the location of the island of Monte Cristo? Why? Can you fix Elba?
4. Imagine yourself to be Edmond Dantès, and describe, in your own words:
   (*a*) your escape from prison;
   (*b*) how you found the treasure.
5. Complete the following sentences:
   Alexandre Dumas was . . . .
   Any person who communicated with . . . .
   The scratching noise was . . . .
   Edmond and the abbé could . . . .
   He did not sink because ....
   He thought he had been shot, but . . . .
   During the night . . . .
   The smugglers . . . .
   Edmond formed a plan to stay on Monte Cristo. It was . . . .
   When the stone was removed he . . . .
   He found the treasure in . . . .
6. Which do you consider was the most exciting moment in the story? Why?
7. Make a list of any new words you have learned in this lesson.

LESSON 18

PICTURE LESSONS—V

THE ALCHYMIST

HERE is a picture full of interesting things.

First of all we notice the man who gives the title to the picture. He is an alchymist.

The chemists or druggists whom we know sell chemicals and medicines in well-lit, clean shops. The alchymists of old spent their lives trying to discover among other things, the elixir of life, which would make people live for ever, and the philosopher's stone, which would change base metals such as lead into gold!

The picture shows the inside of the alchymist's laboratory or workshop. It is a very dark place, but the artist has shown us the alchymist and his jars, jugs, and other odds and ends which he uses in his experiments, in "full light." That is why our eye is attracted to them at once.

We next notice an old man working near a window, who is sitting in what is called a "half light." If we look carefully we shall see that there is another person in the workshop. Do you see him? Perhaps he is a boy apprentice. He is in "complete shadow," and we cannot make out what he is doing.

By means of those three different lights the artist is able to direct our attention to the different parts of his picture in the order of their importance. At the same time the difference of lighting prevents monotony in the picture.

THE ALCHYMIST. (*Van Oslade, 1610–85. National Gallery, London.*)

We could spend a long time examining the objects grouped round about the fireplace. How cleverly the artist has painted them! Notice the large old book in the foreground. It contains the directions for the mixtures of chemicals which the alchymist uses in his experiments.

On the three-legged stool are a clay pipe and a pair of spectacles. Hanging high up is an hour-glass used by the alchymist for timing his experiments—for he lived before clocks and watches were in general use.

Above the hour-glass is a large bucket, hanging near the ceiling. At the right side of the fireplace hangs an old-fashioned wooden shovel on which the artist has signed his name, and the date of the picture: A. V. Ostade, 1661.

It would take too long to point out all the things in the picture. There are many things which you can find out for yourself—such as the basket, the sieve, several crucibles, a tin filler, a ladle, and a broken plate!

It will be noticed that though the picture is mostly painted with dark, dull colours, there are some very bright red parts in it. The two principal red parts are the alchymist's shirt sleeves and a large jar to the right.

There are smaller bright red things scattered about the picture. These red "accents," as they are called, did not happen by chance. The artist put them just where they are to give "warmth" and interest to the whole picture.

The two largest red accents, which are the shirt sleeves and large jar, are repeated by the smaller red accents for the purpose of colour harmony. They are like echoes which repeat more faintly the original sound.

What feeling does the expression on the alchymist's face suggest to you?

LESSON 19

LIMES AND LIME-JUICE

THE lime is a fruit well known to all boys and girls in the West Indies, for most people have at least one lime tree in their garden. You have probably used it to make a refreshing drink, and also for many domestic purposes, such as cleaning pots and pans.

The tree belongs to the same family of plants as the orange, the grape-fruit, the citron, the shaddock, and the lemon, all of which are known by the general name of citrus fruits, and all of which are pulpy fruits with a thick rind. The lime, however, is a more distinctly tropical plant than the others, which flourish even in southern Europe, where the lime will not grow.

There are sweet and sour limes, but the latter kind is the one more generally cultivated. This lime was probably introduced into our lands from the far East, as the tree is found growing wild on the southern slopes of the Himalayas. It seems well adapted to certain parts of the West Indies, where it is now cultivated to a much greater extent than in its original home. The date of its introduction is not recorded, but it is supposed to have been brought here by the Spaniards, and to have found its way to the English islands from the French colony of Martinique. In the *Natural History of Jamaica,* written in 1688, the writer states that the lime was found in his time throughout the island of Jamaica.

The cultivation of the lime on a large scale was first begun in the island of Montserrat, which soon became the headquarters of the lime industry in the West Indies. The lime plantations there, however, have never entirely recovered from the destructive hurricane which swept over that island in 1899, and of late years the larger island of Dominica has produced more limes than any other island. Unfortunately her lime trees have lately been attacked by a disease known as "wither-tip," which is very difficult to stamp out and which may restrict her lime trade. Other islands in which the fruit is grown on a commercial scale are Trinidad, St. Lucia, Antigua, and Grenada.

It is interesting to note that it was the development of machinery and manufactures in Europe about the middle of last century which was responsible for the birth of this agricultural industry in the West Indies. The invention of machines in the cotton trade increased considerably the output of cotton goods. This led to a greater demand for citric acid, which is largely used in the process of dyeing cotton cloth, as well as for other chemical purposes. The juice of the lime contains a large proportion of this acid—more, in fact, than any other species of citrus fruit. Hence efforts were made to supply the demand by growing limes on a large scale. This is a good example to show how events in one part of the world have their effect on the lives and conditions of people in places far removed.

Flat or gently undulating lands, such as those near the coast in Dominica, are regarded as the best for lime cultivation. Limes can also be grown successfully on fairly steep slopes, especially where the land is fed with vegetable matter from forest land above, but not where there are heavy rains, on account of "wither-tip" disease.

Protection from strong winds by "wind-breaks" is a point which needs careful consideration, as lime trees that are exposed to the full force of high winds are often dwarfed and stunted. The flowers are easily blown from the trees, and much loss may result from this, since the principal flushes of flowers occur in February and March, when the winds are liable to be very strong.

The plants can be grown from seed, but on account of root disease among seedlings it is found better to make all fresh plantings with West Indian limes budded on sour orange stock, which is strongly resistant to root disease. The trees are planted from twelve to sixteen feet apart, or twenty-five feet on level land with the best soil conditions.

Although a good lime plantation produces one principal crop annually, there are generally small quantities of fruit to be collected throughout the year. The main crop is gathered from June or July to November or December. The fruits that ripen at this period are produced from flowers which make their appearance from February to June, so that an interval of four to six months is required for the development of the fruit from the flowering stage to the ripening.

The produce of a lime estate is exported in a number of different forms. For shipping as fresh or green limes, the fruits must be picked from the trees as they reach their full growth, and just before the process of ripening begins. These fruits are generally ripe and yellow when they reach their journey's end in Europe or America, where they are used for making refreshing drinks or for flavouring food.

Limes that are intended to be exported as a manufactured product are allowed to ripen on the trees, the fruits when full-ripe dropping to the ground. They are collected by women and girls, and placed in heaps ready to be carried to the mill. The essential oil of limes, known as "ecuelled oil," "hand-pressed oil," or "otto of limes," is obtained from the skins by pressing the limes by hand against blunt spikes before they are crushed in the mill. This oil is more valuable and commands a higher price on the market than the distilled oil which comes from the mill.

Mill for crushing Limes.

There the juice is squeezed from the fruit by heavy granite rollers, or by wooden rollers covered with sheets of copper. The juice must be kept clean and be carefully strained before being put into casks for shipment. In some cases it is boiled to remove a large part of the water, and it is then called concentrated juice.

Another process is the preparation of citrate of lime, in which form the raw lime-juice is brought into combination with some form of chalk. By this means the essential citric acid can be marketed in a more convenient form. This process has now to a large extent displaced the manufacture of concentrated juice.

Fresh lime-juice is made into a refreshing and pleasant drink called cordial. Montserrat lime-juice cordial is known all over the world. The fruit, too, is being used more and more instead of the lemon, especially in America. As we have read earlier in the lesson, the citric acid obtained from the juice is used in the dyeing and calico-printing industries. Lime fruit juice is often given to sailors on long voyages to prevent scurvy, a disease caused by living on salted provisions. It is also said to be good in cases of fever.

Exercises

1. Why are some limes taken from the trees while green, whereas others are allowed to ripen and fall from the trees?
2. What words in the lesson have a similar meaning to the following:

   condensed, taken the place of, made smaller, use in the house, work on the land, changing the colour, rolling, attempts, deep thought, left open, native place.
3. Explain how it is that one cannot fully understand West Indian conditions by studying the West Indies alone. Illustrate your answer by reference to the lime industry.
4. Fill in the missing words in the following passages:

   (*a*) When the plantation is being ——, a good system of roads should be ——, for lime —— are a bulky ——, and they have to be carted to the ——.

   (*b*) The seeds should be washed before being ——. When they are sown un ——, rats very often —— them out and destroy ——; whereas if they are carefully —— and dried, —— but seldom interfere with them.

(c) During heavy ——, which occasionally —— over the islands in the hurricane ——, it sometimes happens that a —— of trees are loosened in the soil, whilst others are —— over.

5. During the year 1926 the exports of lime products from the West Indies were as shown in this table:

	Antigua.	Dominica.	Grenada.	Montserrat.	St. Lucia.	Trinidad.
Lime-juice (raw), galls.	2,950	268,760	—	31,184	43,893	—
„ „ (concen.), galls.	2,050	104,014	6,520	—	35,234	7,886
„ Oil „	—	42,852	284	—	1,661	431
„ Citrate, lb.	—	—	—	3,696	—	—
Limes (green), barrels	87	21,171	—	100	2,810	497

Study these figures, and then arrange the six colonies in their order of importance in the lime trade.

In which colony is the citrate process used? Where do they concentrate most of the juice obtained, and in which island is very little concentrated?

LESSON 20

WHY WATER TORTOISES ARE LARGER THAN LAND TORTOISES

An African Folk-Tale

I

Formerly the kings of Calabar governed all creatures within their territory, from the footless fish to the many-legged centipede. If the sovereign was strong, peace prevailed; but under a weak ruler the beasts, following man's bad example, wrangled among themselves.

Therefore, when Eyamba the Wise became king, he determined to enforce order, and proclaimed that all unnecessary fighting must cease. Any man who disobeyed would be executed; for offending animals, the punishment was death by poisoned arrows, fire, traps, and similar devices.

Knowing that Eyamba could not be trifled with, the beasts reformed so far that they no longer attacked one another, except for the purpose of procuring food.

Nevertheless, many years of quarrelling had soured their tempers, and though the king's rules were not openly broken, the forest resounded with yelping, snarling, neighing, trumpeting, barking, roaring, bellowing, baying, grunting, spitting, screaming, squealing, squeaking, chattering, crowing, squawking, hooting, screeching, gobbling, quacking, cackling, buzzing, humming, croaking, hissing, and rattling, till life was a burden to quiet creatures.

Of all these, the tortoise* suffered most, because he is peculiarly silent and peaceable. For this reason, indeed, he has contrived a small hut, which he carries with him everywhere; so that, when he chooses, he can retire into it and think quietly.

Owing to this habit, practised through a very long life, the tortoise has become a wise and shrewd beast, little as he looks it. At the same time, in spite of his innocent appearance, he is also a bit of a rogue.

One afternoon Udo, the tortoise chief, was sitting at the mouth of his burrow under a prickly tie-tie palm—a tree favoured by his kind, because it keeps away chattering monkeys and other pests. It so happened that some twenty

* *Morocoy* in Creole French patois.

elephants, following Okuni, a huge tusker, came into the clearing near-by, and, after they had fed noisily, began to discuss the jungle doings. Up and down they tramped; the ground quaked beneath them, and their trumpetings set every leaf astir.

Gradually the tortoise became annoyed, and at the end of several hours he had grown quite angry. Taking advantage of a lull in the hubbub, he crawled from under the tie-tie, placed himself before Okuni, and shouted, "A word with you, Windbag!"

Now an elephant's sight is not very sharp, and, though his huge ears serve him better, he relies chiefly on his keen scent. The monster's little, red-rimmed eyes blinked high overhead, while he snuffed indignantly with outstretched trunk. Guided by the acrid smell of the tortoise, he soon spied Udo.

Swinging his trunk aloft, Okuni thundered, "Miserable four-footed snail! how dare you address me so?"

"Lower your tone and your absurd trunk," replied the tortoise. "Let me tell you, once and for all, I will endure no more of your noisy gossiping, which is worse than monkey chatter. Remove yourself and your people at once!"

Okuni raised one of his enormous front feet, saying, "This is my answer!"

But the thick, grey pillar thundered on empty ground, for the tortoise had nimbly retreated into the shelter of the tie-tie.

Okuni's trunk probed the prickly tangle to no purpose; and all the while he could hear his enemy laughing.

"Listen, Little Wit!" called out Udo, "it is not wise to provoke me further, since I am stronger than you."

OKUNI THUNDERED, "MISERABLE FOUR-FOOTED SNAIL! HOW DARE YOU ADDRESS ME SO?"

(*See page 104.*)

Okuni's huge ears stiffened with surprise; and when he answered, his tone was much less confident. "Surely the gods have deprived you of your senses! How can so puny a beast as you pretend to be a match for me, the strongest of all the forest people?"

"Your vanity deceives you," replied the tortoise. "Strength is not to be measured by bulk. As I have no relish for one of Eyamba's traps or poisoned arrows, we cannot fight; but, if you dare, we will have a trial to prove which is the stronger. These are the terms. Let each be fastened to one end of a suitable rope; then, before witnesses, I shall go down into my bathing pool, while you remain on the bank. At a given signal, you must try to draw me out. That, I wager one thousand ripe yams, you will be unable to do."

The herd could hardly believe their enormous ears, and some of them thought it was beneath their leader's dignity to accept such a challenge. However, after discussion, the trial was fixed for the following day, and the giants departed noisily.

When Udo retired into his burrow he found his wife in tears. She had been listening, and cried so bitterly that huge tears splashed into the coo-coo, while she stirred it for their meal. Shrill with anger, she told Udo that the loss of a thousand yams would ruin his family. At this the youngsters wailed and wept.

Udo tried to reassure them, saying that he had no fear as to the result, but no one believed him. That night some very wet little tortoises sobbed themselves to sleep; and the wife, wakeful through anxiety, was almost driven mad by hearing her husband chuckle continually to himself in the darkness.

News of the wager spread over the forest, and by the next afternoon the banks of the pool were crowded. Millions of birds occupied the tree tops; half the lower branches bent under the weight of monkeys, packed close as corn on a cob. Below, jostled herds of animals, overtopped by great grey shapes, the elephant clan; and the hot air rang with every jungle sound.

Near the edge of the pool stood Okuni, waiting for the tortoise, who presently crawled up, accompanied by his brother. Between them they were carrying a long, stout rope of tie-tie fibre, stolen from a riverside village.

The leopard had been asked to umpire. He fastened one end of the cable about the elephant's neck, the other round that of the tortoise; called for silence, and gave out the conditions. Udo was to dive in, and, when ready, jerk the rope thrice as a signal the tug might begin.

These matters settled, Okuni turned his back to the pool, into which the tortoise plunged. Countless eyes—black, yellow, grey, green, blue, golden, silvery—watched him disappear; and as the waters smoothed themselves out, all, even the monkeys, were silent. Thrice the rope shook, and the elephant, standing squarely with his head turned backwards, saw the umpire's paw flash aloft as a signal that all was ready. At once Okuni flung his whole weight into the pull.

The struggle had begun!

When the water closed on him, Udo swam towards a deep hollow, across which, as he knew, lay a great sunken tree. Round this he tied the cable, then, after giving three strong jerks, settled himself on the slime to watch the result. The heavy trunk stirred in its bed; once it lifted, but only to settle again in the upchurned ooze; then suddenly the rope slackened and sank to the bottom of the pool.

Quickly untying the end, Udo gripped it between his jaws and scrambled out into the sunshine. A storm of mingled cries saluted him, for a strange thing had happened!

At the signal Okuni had flung all his weight and sinew into the pull; but in spite of all his efforts he could not advance the breadth of a blade of grass. Goaded by fear of defeat, he made a final effort; the hawser snapped, and Okuni turned a complete somersault between his vast outspread ears.

The giant scrambled to his feet, and stood quivering with shame and deafened by gusts of sound, above which rang the bark of the monkeys, who swung and gambolled aloft, gibbering delightedly, till their fierce enemy, the leopard, climbed a tree and cuffed a dozen of the mockers into terrified stillness.

All the lesser animals congratulated Udo, but the larger ones held sulkily aloof, and departed, following the example of Okuni, who slunk off in silence with his tribe. Elephants are honourable beasts, and, in spite of the danger run by those who broke Eyamba's strict laws against theft, next morning a thousand ripe yams lay piled round the tie-tie palm.

II

Now Isantim, the hippopotamus, and his people had always been friends of the elephants, partly because they were distant relations, and also for the reason that, as one tribe lived on land and the other in pools, lakes, or rivers, there was no rivalry between them. He therefore felt the slight put on Okuni, especially as the monkeys took pains to inform him that Udo was boasting he could out-dive any hippopotamus in Calabar.

This report worried Isantim so much that the juiciest river plants hardly tempted him to feed. As he wallowed in the mud he often murmured: "Stone Coat must be mad! I have met him in the water, and his pace was a mere crawl compared with mine. The reptile is beneath my notice."

One day, as the hippopotamus was floating in his favourite haunt, a deep creek by the river, Udo appeared on the bank, and shouted insolently: "Greetings, Isantim! You grow fatter every day! Perhaps you hope that, by so doing, no jaw will be wide enough to gain a hold on you; for certainly, if you were attacked, you could not save yourself by speed or nimbleness."

Isantim opened his vast pink mouth and laughed. "Forgive me, Friend Bandy Legs," he said, with mock politeness, "but your words amuse me, seeing that on land you are none too speedy, and still less so in the water."

"Come, come! Floating Gourd!" replied Udo jauntily. "Though I do not pretend to swim as fast as an alligator, I can beat you with ease, especially at diving."

Isantim laughed again, but in a very half-hearted fashion.

"Listen!" continued the impudent reptile. "You deserve, and shall receive, a lesson. I am going home to feed my family, but propose to return before long, and make good my words, by challenging you to dive across this creek for one thousand ripe yams a side. As I have no wish to shame you in public, I suggest we decide the matter quietly, without any spectators."

"Agreed!" answered the hippopotamus faintly. "You will find me here."

The tortoise shuffled off. Isantim waded out of the creek, and lay down in the mud to rest, so that he might be fresher for the coming trial. As the moments passed he grew more and more nervous, and snorted so loudly that even the flies did not venture to approach him.

After the midday meal Udo called on his brother, and led him a little way into the forest. The two had been hatched from the same cluster of eggs, and, even when they stood side by side, it was almost impossible to tell them apart. Udo spoke in a whisper. As he did so the brother nodded approval, and at last laughed aloud.

"Silence!" said Udo hastily. "Reserve your mirth for this evening. You must be off at once. I shall give you an hour's start; and mind you keep under cover as much as possible."

The brother left at a brisk pace. Udo rested awhile before returning to the creek, where he found Isantim sprawling on the mud in the sunshine. As soon as Udo appeared, the hippopotamus came lumbering ashore.

Side by side they stood on the bank, and they could hardly look at the glare of the water.

"There is no time to lose," remarked Udo. "If you are ready, let us begin. Now as to the conditions. The first across to yonder palm wins. Secondly; once we are below the surface, neither is to rise above it till the other side is reached. Whoever does so, loses. In this matter we must, of course, rely on each other's honour."

"Exactly," grunted Isantim. "But what about the start?"

"Why," answered the tortoise, "suppose you say, 'One, two, three, off!' At the last word, in we go. Are you ready?"

Isantim thrice filled and emptied his huge lungs, barked out the signal, took a vast breath, clashed his jaws together, and hurtled through the rushes, disappearing under a heave of water that washed up the bank to the very grass.

Udo dived also, but, once below, instead of heading across, turned about and came up noiselessly in a bed of tall reeds, among which he lay securely screened.

Meanwhile Isantim wallowed on at top speed deep under water. It was such a long dive that his chest was near to bursting when he felt the bottom under his feet, and, through a wash of liquid mud, lurched ashore into the shadow of the trees on the farther bank.

There, fronting him, stood the tortoise, quite unruffled. At once the odious reptile cried:

"I am glad you have turned up at last. Really, I began to fear you were drowned, and the thought of your bereaved family was distressing me."

Dumb and breathless, Isantim glared at his conqueror, who continued—

"I presume you do not care for a second trial. Ah! I thought not. As it is a warm evening, I shall dive again for the sake of coolness. My poor, stout friend, when you have rested, float over at your leisure. You will find me waiting."

With a splash he disappeared in the twilit creek. After a while Isantim paddled back and floundered out, uttering so deep a sigh that the mud quivered, for there, on the grass, the tortoise sat quietly in the dim light.

"Convinced, I think," he called out to the shamefaced monster. "But how did you imagine that, with such a build as yours, it was possible for you to beat me? I am sorry you are tired. Pleasant dreams to you!"

Isantim tramped sadly to his lair by the river. All night he rolled and splashed among the reeds, with star-gleams a-twinkle on his puzzled, sleepless eyes.

The victor walked some distance, and then halted for an hour or so; at the end of which time another tortoise came shuffling through the twilit gloom. They greeted each other warmly.

"Splendid, brother!" said Udo. "You played your part well. Between us we might form a little society which would rule the forest. I promise you a good supper and a hundred ripe yams; but we had better return separately, for fear any inquisitive eyes should be spying on us."

A few days later, impressed by their experiences, Okuni and Isantim begged the tortoise to dwell with them, and protect them against their enemies. At first Udo refused, but they pressed him, and finally he decided to live with the elephants on land, suggesting that, as he could not be in two places at once, his brother should inhabit the water with the hippopotamus.

The proposal was accepted, and worked well; but as fish is more plentiful and sustaining than berries or other forest produce, in course of time it came about that water tortoises have developed into a much larger and plumper breed than the land variety; and so, in all likelihood, they will continue to be.

From "Folk-Tales of the Nations."

Exercises

1. Study the verbal nouns *(quarrelling,* etc.) in the third paragraph of p. 103. How many are there? What others could you give describing noises made by any class of animals?
2. Make a list of the animals of the mammal class mentioned in this lesson. What other classes of animals are mentioned in the tale? Give the names of any of those classes.
3. What is a "folk-tale"? Where have you read any other folk-tales? Do you know of another folk-tale in which the elephant and the hippopotamus are beaten by a weaker animal? In this case it was a rabbit.
4. In what other tale does the tortoise appear? Is he successful in that tale too?
5. What plants which grow in the West Indies are named in this lesson?
6. Make a list of twelve words from the lesson which cause you difficulty in their spelling.
7. Make sentences of your own containing these phrases:

    could not be trifled with — accompanied by his brother
    life was a burden — turned a complete somersault
    his innocent appearance — in spite of the danger
    to no purpose — stood side by side
    to be a match — rely on each other's honour

8. Which, in your opinion, was the more clever device: when Udo beat Okuni, or when he hoodwinked Isantim? Give reasons for your choice.

THE BUCCANEERS.

LESSON 21

THE BUCCANEERS—I

FOR many years after their discovery the islands of the West Indies remained in the possession of Spain. At that time Spain was the great colonizing power—as colonizing was then understood. As a pioneer and discoverer she was closely rivalled by her neighbour Portugal, and in the year 1498 (that of the third voyage of Columbus) Vasco da Gama, one of her navigators, had rounded the Cape of Good Hope and discovered a new route to India.

About this time the Pope, influenced by the powerful King Ferdinand of Spain, is said to have sent for a map of the world, and then, drawing a line from pole to pole through the middle of the Atlantic, he solemnly bestowed on the King of Spain all the lands that should be discovered to the west of that line, and on the King of Portugal all those to the east. The Portuguese objected, and a year later this arrangement was altered by treaty, the line being shifted westwards, giving to the Portuguese the eastern portion of Brazil.

With this exception, Spain in the sixteenth century (1500–1600) claimed the whole of America. Westward ho! sailed her galleons, following in the track of Columbus, and bearing to the heathen the blessing of civilization. But ever their quest was for gold, and rivers of gold poured into the treasury of Spain as the well-filled ships, returning from her West Indian possessions, brought untold wealth wrung from the peaceful folk of the islands, of Mexico, and of Peru.

Meantime England had grown to be her deadly foe, since no Englishman would listen for a moment to the claim of King Philip II. of Spain to be England's king, although he had married Mary, the Queen of England. There had also appeared of late years a band of English adventurers—"Buccaneers," as the Spaniards afterwards called them—who were by no means inclined to leave undisputed the claim of Spain to be Mistress of the Seas, and who were beginning to take a share in searching out new lands in the west.

Rollicking sea-dogs they were, with their peaked beards, sunburnt faces, and keen bright eyes, each eager to dare the perils of the deep, to "singe the King of Spain's beard" and to plunder his oversea dominions. It was a kind of "private warfare" they carried on, as their acts could be disowned by their country when necessary. Nevertheless, the English rovers were in their own eyes fighting for freedom; the more they harried the West Indies, the more gold they captured, so much the more did they hamper Spain in Europe and make it difficult for her to pay her troops in the Netherlands, which had revolted against her, and so prevent the invasion of England desired by her king.

For a time Elizabeth, England's queen, who had succeeded her sister Mary, encouraged and assisted them secretly, and managed to avert open warfare with Spain until she felt her people were prepared and her ships ready. Then she openly incited her seamen to plunder the Spanish ships and coast towns. No fewer than five of her foremost "sea-dogs" were men of Devon, and one and all had pluck enough to take the Whole responsibility of their adventures, receiving the queen's rebukes as a matter of course if things went amiss, and sharing with her the profits if all went well.

All on this side to belong to Spain. ← → *All on this side to belong to Portugal.*

One of them, Sir John Hawkins, having heard of the slave-trade carried on by Spain, sailed to Africa, shipped a number of natives, and boldly sold them, under the very eyes of the Spaniards, to the settlers in the West Indies, where they were put to work on the sugar and tobacco plantations.

Hawkins.

With him on his third expedition went his kinsman, Francis Drake, a lad of twenty-one, who put all the little money of which he was possessed into the undertaking. But by this time King Philip was on the alert, and determined to punish these daring adventurers. The Spanish fleet was out on their track, and of the little company of English ships all were sunk except the two commanded by Hawkins and Drake themselves, which only escaped with the greatest difficulty.

This misadventure helped to make Drake the lifelong enemy of Spain; and as he had been ruined by it, he determined that his enemy should dearly pay the cost. From this time he became the dreaded "El Draco"—the dragon of the Spanish Seas.

In 1572 Drake set out with two little ships, with the daring intent of robbing the town of Nombre de Dios on the Isthmus of Panama, in which the Spaniards stored the rich treasure brought from Mexico and Peru, and from which it was shipped to Spain. Landing as near the town as possible, Drake said to his men, "I have now brought you to the treasury of the world. If you fail to take what you want, you alone are to blame." But in the fight for the rich spoil the leader was so severely wounded, that, to his deep disgust, his men left the treasure-house untouched, and carried him off by force to a place of safety.

Drake.

As soon as he had recovered he determined to seize the next convoy of treasure that was brought to the town; and it was while he marched inland for this purpose that the event took place which later on had much to do with the growth of the British Empire, as it led him to explore the Pacific and sail round the world. Let one of his fellow-voyagers tell the tale:

"After travelling several days," he says, "we came to a high hill lying east and west between the two seas (the Atlantic and Pacific oceans). Here was a great and goodly tree, and from the top we might see the ocean we came from (the Atlantic) and the ocean we so much desired. After our captain had seen that sea, of which he had heard such golden reports, he besought Almighty God of His goodness to give him life and leave to sail once in an English ship on that sea."

DRAKE RECEIVING THE HONOUR OF KNIGHTHOOD FROM QUEEN ELIZABETH.

From the day of Hawkins and Drake, then, the sunlit West Indian seas became the haunt of the English seamen-adventurers; the Spanish Main was the goal of all their ambitions; there, war or no war, they smote their mortal foes, the Spanish Dons, whenever and wherever they were met. In our seas were trained the English mastiffs that worried to death the great Spanish Armada; and here in our waters sleeps Francis Drake, one of the greatest of English sea-captains, with many another gallant sailor.

Exercises

1. Explain why the only Portuguese colony in South America was Brazil.
2. Study the map on page 117. Who was the first European sailor to round Cape Horn? Who sailed up the west coast of South America? Where did he go after that?
3. Why did Spain desire lands in the New World? Why was England her deadly foe?
4. Who were the buccaneers? Why did they come to the West Indies?
5. Who was Sir John Hawkins? What did he do?
6. Give an account of the work of Sir Francis Drake in this part of the world.
7. Make a list of twelve words in this lesson which cause you difficulty to spell.
8. Fill in the blanks:
   (*a*) By men of British race all the world over, the name West —— is held dear, for it was in those —— that the foundations of the British —— were ——.
   (*b*) In the —— —— and off the Spanish —— her —— learnt their seamanship and navigation which served them in good stead in their struggle with the great —— —— in the English Channel.

(*c*) In the time of Queen —— the Spaniards said that all the ——beyond the —— Ocean belonged to ——, because the —— sailors had been the —— to discover America.

(*d*) The men of —— set —— for the Spanish seas, and boldly attacked the great —— ships. Sometimes the English "—— ——", as they were called, even attacked the —— ports and seized the —— as it was lying on the ——.

(*e*) The queen was —— of her sailors, and wore in her crown some of the —— they brought back.

LESSON 22

WEEDS

In garden work one is often asked, "Would you please tell me if this is a weed?" Sometimes the question is not easy to answer, because weeds do not belong to any particular family of plants. What is called a weed in the vegetable garden may be a cultivated plant in the flower garden.

If I were asked what I understand by the term weed, I would say that a weed is a plant that is not wanted in the particular place where it happens to be growing. If, for example, you were growing in your garden a nice bed of zinnias, and you found springing up amongst them seedlings of grass and other plants which had occupied the bed previously, you would treat all except the zinnias as weeds, and pull them out. They would all be plants out of their proper place, making the garden beds untidy and robbing the cultivated plants of their food. The name "weed" is commonly applied to wild plants which invade cultivated ground, but it is better to regard it in this wider sense.

Although there are some plants, such as nut grass, which we always regard as weeds, it would be a difficult task to give a general list of them. Some are very useful when growing where they are wanted, as, for example, savannah grass, devil or Bermuda grass, and many other grasses which make good lawns and furnish fodder for animals. They may, however, be bad weeds when growing in paths or in the flower or vegetable garden.

Nut Grass.

The destruction of weeds is the principal work in the garden, and on their proper control depends the success or failure of the cultivated plants. Weeding is sometimes regarded as drudgery, but it is very necessary garden work, and must be diligently attended to.

Weeds do harm to cultivated plants in several ways. Their roots absorb much of the moisture and plant food in the soil, and their stems and leaves shade the cultivated plants and rob them of the sunlight which is essential for their growth.

Many plants which are generally called weeds are really very beautiful and suitable for cultivation, but owing to prejudice are scarcely ever seen in gardens. A good story is told by a well-known man who had a pretty little wild plant growing in a pot. One day a visitor admired it very much and inquired of what nurseryman it could be obtained. On explaining that it was a native plant and could be found growing wild quite close to his house, the visitor said, "Oh, I did not know it was only a weed," and took no further interest in it.

The sensitive plant is a pretty weed which interests children, and even older persons, on account of the movements it makes when touched. I have even seen it grown in pots in glass-houses in Europe, where it is considered a great curiosity for the same reason. It is, however, one of the worst weeds in our West Indian pastures.

Sensitive Plant.

Some weeds are edible; several of the spinaches, or bahje, are often gathered and cooked for food.

Weeds or wild plants sometimes serve a useful purpose by giving us an idea of the suitability for agricultural purposes of the land in which they are growing, as, for example, the gru-gru palm on poor hillsides. According to the nature of the weeds so we may often judge as to whether the soil is good or bad. When growing among crop plants they are often the means of reminding us that the surface soil needs stirring; this is therefore done when the land is hoed and the weeds are destroyed.

Weeds usually produce seeds in large numbers, and since we have seen how many means there are by which these may be spread, the abundance of weeds in the garden can readily be understood. Wind is the usual means of their dispersal, and if there are any gardens or lands in a neglected condition, it is not surprising that there are plenty of weeds on the neighbouring plots. The seeds may also come from long distances, or be brought by birds or animals or in manure.

English Glass-house.

All weeds are not propagated by seeds. Sometimes when hoeing garden beds we chop plants like the cockroach grass into pieces, and if the weather be moist these pieces will often grow. The little hard nuts on the roots of the nut grass will form new plants, and in cleaning beds it is necessary to dig up the entire plants and burn them. Merely chopping off the tops will not kill them.

When new kinds of plants are introduced into a country it is necessary to watch them to see that they do not become troublesome weeds. Although plants are not always weeds in their native country, they may become such in the land of their adoption. A West Indian native plant known as clidemia, which was supposed to have been introduced into Fiji by means of coffee from Brazil, is now a troublesome weed in its new home. In the wet belt of Fiji it is reported to cover thousands of acres, to the exclusion of all other vegetation. It is so troublesome that it is known as "Koster's curse." Although this plant is fairly common in some of our islands, it certainly cannot be said to be a troublesome weed. This, therefore, is a case where the conditions in the country of its adoption are more favourable to its growth than those in its native land.

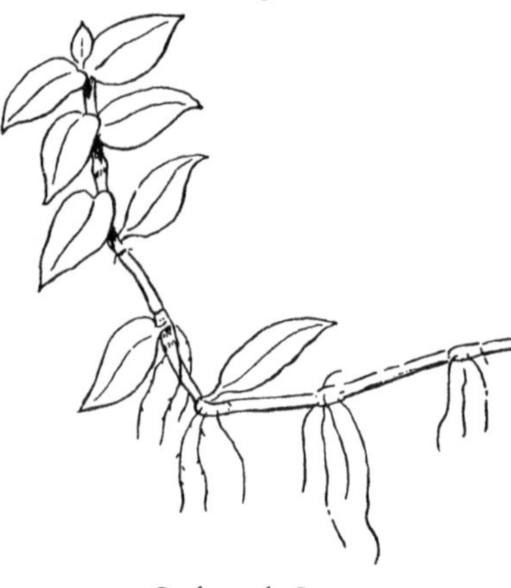
Cockroach Grass.

Other West Indian native plants which have been introduced into Ceylon are now found there as bad weeds; examples are the sensitive plant and tithonia. The wild sage is also an alien plant to Ceylon, yet it is the most prevalent weed in that country.

Oats and other grain frequently contain weed seeds mixed with them; the thistle has become a pest in some countries through its introduction in this way.

A common way of destroying weeds is to hoe the land, but in the case of those with persistent underground stems or other similar structures they must be dug up and burnt. Hoeing should be done frequently in order that the weeds may not have time to produce ripe seeds, otherwise more will grow in a very short time.

There are other methods besides working the soil which are used by some people for killing weeds. These usually consist of watering them with some poisonous chemical, when they quickly die. These chemicals are known as weed-killers, and many different kinds are sold for the purpose. They are, however, only used on roads and paths, as they will, of course, kill cultivated plants as well. Salt or strong brine will also kill weeds.

In this lesson you have learned the harm that weeds can do, and also that some are useful and beautiful. We shall always have weeds in our gardens, but it is our own fault if they kill the cultivated plants, as we know several ways in which they may be destroyed.

Exercises

1. What do you mean by a weed? Give examples to illustrate your answer.
2. In what ways are weeds useful to us?
3. Some weeds are beautiful or interesting plants, yet they are not cultivated. Why?
4. Suppose your garden had many weeds in it, what might be the cause, or causes, of their presence?
5. Make sentences of your own containing these words:

essential	suitability	persistent
cultivated (*adj.*)	propagated	chemicals
diligently	favourable	entire
stirring	conditions	prevalent

6. Give the *opposites* of the following:

alien	frequently	strong
abundance	quickly	taking
neglected	different	beautiful
harmful	many	previously

7. Fill in the blanks:
   (*a*) A —— gardener always tries to —— weeds, as they —— the growth of his ——.
   (*b*) The kind of —— which grows in a particular —— may often show the —— of the soil.
   (*c*) Weeds with —— stems are very difficult to ——, as they must be completely —— up and ——.
   (*d*) Manure often contains —— of weeds, so that they may be —— into the garden by this means.
   (*e*) Weeds do —— to —— plants, as they rob them of the ——, ———, ———, and —— which they need.
8. Make drawings of any of the specimens of weeds in the Nature-study collection in your school. If there is not such a collection, you should start to make one.
9. Where are the following places? Find them on a map of the world: Fiji, Brazil, and Ceylon.

LESSON 23

PICTURE LESSONS—VI

A Lonely Life

You will probably agree that the title of the picture on page 131 describes it very aptly. Here we see an old woman of the Highlands of Scotland returning to her cottage at the end of the day. In one arm she carries a bundle of sticks which she has gathered on her way home, and which she will use for her evening fire. She has set down her provision basket at her feet while she unlocks her door.

There is no one to welcome her on her return—not even a dog or a cat to bark or purr when she appears in sight: truly "a lonely life."

The arrangement or composition of the picture and its painting are as simple as the subject itself. Consider how little there is in the picture: a humble old woman and part of the outside of her poor cottage, with a little bit of sky and distant hill; and yet the painting tells its story fully and effectively.

The artist might have put many other appropriate things into his picture, such as a garden, or trees, or even other houses. Do you think that those things which might have been quite natural in such a scene would have helped him in telling his story of "a lonely life"?

The artist has put in only what was absolutely necessary, and this helps to create the feeling of loneliness, and to arouse our pity for the old woman.

Let us notice carefully how he has treated the few Components of his picture. Instead of making the different parts stand out clearly and separately from one another, he has blended them together in a wonderful way. Only the old woman's head and hands stand out clearly against the light colour of the cottage wall; all the rest of the picture is shadowy and indistinct except the distant hill crowned with a rosy cloud.

The upper part of the picture is mostly light, the lower part mostly dark. We can just see the lower part of the woman's figure, the basket, and the edge of the seat against the cottage wall, and we must imagine the road in front of the cottage, which disappears into the dark distance.

See how soft and tender the painting of the picture is. There are no hard, sharp, precise outlines anywhere—everything is soft and mysterious. Pictures of this kind are seen at their best if looked at from a distance. Hold this one about three feet away and note the effect.

There is a small window suggested at the right side of the cottage wall, and we cannot tell where the house ends and the landscape background begins. This is not carelessness on the part of the artist, but part of his plan.

The painter has used only a very few colours in painting his picture, brown and grey of light and dark tones being the principal ones. He has, however, used a dull red for the woman's shawl, dull green for her skirt, and a brighter green for the cottage door.

This picture shows us that a true artist is not only a good painter, but also a sympathetic story-teller. He is not so much concerned to show us how clever he is with palette and brush, as to present before us the chosen incident in such a way as to rouse our interest and our sympathy.

When we look at his picture we forget about the means which the artist employed to make it, and we think only with deep sympathy of the poor old woman who lives such "a lonely life".

A LONELY LIFE.
(Hugh Cameron, R.S.A.,1837–1918. By kind permission of the Trustees of the late Alexander Rose, Glasgow.)

LESSON 24

COCOA AND CHOCOLATE

The Natural History of Chocolate, written by R. Brookes in 1730, contains a description of the preparation of chocolate from the *cacao* bean as practised in early

Raw Cocoa Store, with Mechanical Conveyor, Bournville.
(Photo: Cadbury Brothers, Ltd.)

times. It states: "The Indians, from whom we borrow it, are not very nice in doing it; they roast the kernels in earthen pots, then free them from their skins, and afterwards crush and grind them between two stones, and so form cakes of it with their hands."

In the West Indies even to-day yon may have seen chocolate being prepared in small quantities by peasants who use methods similar to this. These simple processes have, however, undergone many elaborations and refinements in the large factories of Europe and America, where most of the *cacao* we produce is sent for manufacture into cocoa powder and chocolate.

Let us follow the beans to the factory and learn something of the processes they go through after leaving our estates before they return to us in the various forms of cocoa and chocolate we can buy in the stores.

Roasting Cocoa Beans, Bournville.

In the first picture you can see one of the large warehouses where the *cacao* is stored until required. The stocks are, of course, always changing: always there are new arrivals, always the day's requirements passing out. With such a constant traffic you can imagine what an immense help is the endless conveyor shown. As the men unstack the mighty heap the bags fall on to the continuous band which carries them out of the store.

All *cacao* is liable to contain a little free shell, dried pulp, threads of sacking, and other foreign matter, so it is first very carefully sieved and sorted. This is done by a machine somewhat like the rotating sieve which grades stones after they have been crushed in a quarry.

Cocoa Grinding

It produces what the manufacturers desire—a clean bean sorted to size.

Cocoa is similar to coffee in one respect: it is the product of a roasting process which gives it its characteristic flavour and aroma. This roasting is done in revolving cylinders or drums over fire or gas. You can see a number of them in the picture on page 133. As the drums rotate, experienced workmen carefully examine their contents to see that the exact degree of roasting shall be attained which will secure the richest aroma.

The beans then undergo a process called "kibbling," or "breaking down," which not only liberates the husk or shell, but breaks up the bean into fragments known

Chocolate Refining.

as "cocoa nibs" the shell being separated from them by means of a powerful current of air.

They are then roasted, different kinds being treated differently, so as to develop in each its characteristic flavour. The different sorts are blended in proportions which are carefully chosen to attain the desired result. As long ago as 1924 cocoa from Trinidad and Grenada was mixed to form the popular "Trinada" chocolate sold at the great Exhibition at Wembley in England.

The nibs next pass to the grinding mills, where they are crushed and ground several times. The result is not a powder, but a thick paste, owing to the fact that half the bean is fat, or "cocoa butter," which is melted by the heat.

In the manufacture of cocoa powder it is necessary to extract a certain amount of the cocoa butter, and this is done by means of powerful hydraulic presses. This process leaves the cocoa in firm, dry cakes, which are taken from the presses and broken and ground again. It is then passed through fine silk sieves to form the powder which we can buy in tins at the grocery store.

Machines which seem almost human weigh it with remarkable speed and accuracy, and place the required quantity in the paper bag with which each tin is lined. The tins are then labelled and packed in cases ready for export to all parts of the world.

We will now see something of the preparation of chocolate in its various forms. In the manufacture of cocoa a large proportion of the fat is extracted, but this is retained in making eating chocolate. The nibs, coarse or finely ground, are mixed with fine sugar in machines called *melangeurs,* or mixers. You can see some of them in the picture on page 135. They consist of two heavy mill-stones, which, supported on a revolving base, crush and mix the two ingredients as they rotate, the result being a dough-like paste. After more grinding in mills of a different type, this paste becomes a fine powder.

For certain kinds of chocolate, cocoa butter is added to form a soft paste. The chocolate then passes to "conching" machines, so called from their shell-like shape, where it is

Assortment centres being covered with chocolate.

pushed to and fro by heavy rollers, the process giving it the velvety feeling on the palate.

If "plain" chocolate is required, the rich brown mass is conveyed to the moulding departments, where it is run into small tin moulds of varying patterns. When cool and hard, the familiar cakes, tablets, or bars are knocked out and are ready for packing.

Often is the question asked: "How do the creams, the nuts, or those other delicious confections get inside the chocolate?" The answer is that they are covered with chocolate while it is still in the liquid state. The picture on page 137 shows a few of the many girl workers engaged in dipping the confectionery or fruit "centres" into the warm chocolate. Before each girl is a bowl of the chocolate kept at the right temperature, and by means of a fork she dips in the "centres," of which she has a stock at her elbow, and also adds the decoration. We are amazed at how quickly she can do this with her deft hands and light touch.

The many packing-rooms in the factory are also staffed with girls, who weigh and arrange the contents of the various tins and boxes which find their way into all countries of the world.

Exercises

1. Explain the difference between cacao, cocoa, and chocolate.
2. In what respects are cocoa and coffee alike?
3. What is the essential difference between the method employed by the original inhabitants of South America and that of the modern factory in the making of cocoa?
4. What have you learned in this lesson that yon did not know before?
5. If you go through a chocolate factory, what questions would you ask to make clear any points which you do not understand after reading this lesson?
6. Study the pictures in this lesson. Would you like to work in such a factory? If you would, give your reasons; if not, say why not.
7. Why do you think the large chocolate factories are in Europe and America instead of in the West Indies where the cacao is grown?
8. Write out the ten words in this lesson which cause you the most difficulty in their spelling.

LESSON 25

THE CRICKET MATCH

Introduction.—Cricket has become the national game of the West Indies. The exploits of their sons on the savannahs at home, as well as on the fields of England, have made the West Indies famous for cricket throughout the British Commonwealth. I am sure, therefore, all West Indian boys (and girls too) will enjoy reading this lesson, which is one of the finest descriptions of a cricket match ever written.

I hope, too, you will obtain the book *Tom Brown's Schooldays,* to read the whole story of the famous school of Rugby. There we find this picture of Tom Brown on the day of the match: "By his side, in white flannel shirt and trousers, straw hat, the captain's belt, and the untanned yellow cricket shoes, which all the eleven wear, sits a strapping figure, near six feet high, with ruddy, tanned face and whiskers, curly brown hair, and a laughing, dancing eye. He is leaning forward with his elbows resting on his knees, and dandling his favourite bat, with which he has made thirty or forty runs to-day, in his strong brown hands. It is Tom Brown, grown into a young man nineteen years old, a prefect and captain of the eleven, spending his last day as a Rugby boy."

"OH, well bowled! well bowled, Johnson!" cries the captain, catching up the ball and sending it high above the rook trees, while the third Marylebone* man walks away from the wicket, and old Bailey gravely sets up the middle stump again and puts the bails on.

"How many runs?" Away scamper three boys to the scoring-table, and are back again in a minute amongst the rest of the eleven, who are collected together in a knot

* Marylebone Cricket Club (M.C.C.).

between wickets. "Only eighteen runs, and three wickets down!" "Huzza for old Rugby!" sings out Jack Raggles, the long-stop, toughest and burliest of boys—commonly called "Swiper Jack"—and forthwith stands on his head, and brandishes his legs in the air in triumph till the next boy catches hold of his heels and throws him over on to his back.

"Steady, there; don't be such an ass, Jack," says the captain. "We haven't got the best wicket yet. Ah, look out now at cover-point!" adds he, as he sees a long-armed, bare-headed, slashing-looking player coming to the wicket. "And, Jack, mind your hits. He steals more runs than any man in England."

And they all find that they have got their work to do now: the new-comer's off-hitting is tremendous, and his running like a flash of lightning. He is never in his ground, except when his wicket is down. Nothing in the whole game is so trying to boys—he has stolen three byes in the first ten minutes—and Jack Raggles is furious, and begins throwing over savagely to the farther wicket, until he is sternly stopped by the captain. It is all that young gentleman can do to keep his team steady; but he knows that everything depends on it, and faces his work bravely.

The score creeps up to fifty: the boys begin to look blank, and the spectators, who are now mustering strong, are very silent. The ball flies off his bat to all parts of the field, and he gives no rest and no catches to any one. But cricket is full of glorious chances, and the goddess who presides over it loves to bring down the most skilful players.

Johnson, the young bowler, is getting wild, and bowls a ball almost wide to the off; cover-point is standing very deep. The ball comes skimming and twisting along about

AT THE WICKET.

three feet from the ground. He rushes at it, and it sticks somehow or other in the fingers of his left hand, to the utter astonishment of himself and the whole field. Such a catch hasn't been made in the close for years, and the cheering is maddening. "Pretty cricket," says the captain, throwing himself on the ground by the deserted wicket with a long breath; he feels that a crisis has passed.

I wish I had space to describe the whole match: how the captain stumped the next man off a leg-shooter, and bowled slow lobs to old Mr. Aislabie, who came in for the last wicket; how the Lord's* men were out by half-past twelve o'clock for ninety-eight runs; how the captain of the School Eleven went in first to give his men pluck, and scored twenty-five in beautiful style; how Rugby was only four behind in the first innings.

What a glorious dinner they had in the fourth-form School, and how the cover-point hitter sang the most topping comic songs, and old Mr. Aislabie afterwards made the best speeches that ever were heard. But I haven't space, that's the fact; and so you must fancy it all, and carry yourselves on to half-past seven o'clock, when the School are again in, with five wickets down, and only thirty-two runs to make to win. The Marylebone men played carelessly in their second innings, but they are working like horses now to save the match.

. . . .

Meantime Jack Raggles, with his sleeves tucked up above his great brown elbows, scorning pads and gloves, has presented himself at the wicket, and having

* *Lord's*, the home ground of the M.C.C.

run one for a forward drive of Johnson's, is about to receive his first ball. There are only twenty-four runs to make, and four wickets to go down—a winning match if they play decently steady.

The ball is a very swift one, and rises fast, catching Jack on the outside of the thigh, and bounding away as if from india-rubber, while they run two for a leg-bye amidst great applause, and shouts from Jack's many admirers. The next ball is a beautifully-pitched ball for the outer stump, which the reckless and unfeeling Jack catches hold of, and hits right round to leg for five, while the applause becomes deafening. Only seventeen runs to get with four wickets: the game is all but ours!

Jack walks swaggering about his wicket, with the bat over his shoulder, while Mr. Aislabie holds a short parley with his men. Then the cover-point hitter, that cunning man, goes on to bowl slow twisters. Jack waves his hand triumphantly towards the tent, as much as to say, "See if I don't finish it all off now in three hits!"

Alas! my son Jack, the enemy is too old for thee. The first ball of the over Jack steps out and meets, swiping with all his force. If he had only allowed for the twist! But he hasn't, and so the ball goes spinning up straight into the air, as if it would never come down again.

Away runs Jack shouting, and trusting to the chapter of accidents; but the bowler runs steadily under it, judging every spin, and calling out, "I have it!?" catches it, and playfully pitches it on to the back of the stalwart Jack, who is departing with a rueful countenance.

"I knew how it would be," says Tom, rising "Come along; the game's getting very serious."

So they leave the island and go to the tent, and after deep consultation Arthur is sent in, and goes off to the wicket with a last exhortation from Tom to play steady and keep his bat straight. To the suggestion that Winter is the best bat left Tom only replies, "Arthur is the steadiest, and Johnson will make the runs if the wicket is only kept up."

. . . .

The clock strikes eight, and the whole field becomes fevered with excitement. Arthur, after two narrow escapes, scores one; and Johnson gets the ball. The bowling and fielding are superb, and Johnson's batting worthy the occasion. He makes here a two and there a one, managing to keep the ball to himself; and Arthur backs up, and runs perfectly. Only eleven runs to make now, and the crowd scarcely breathes.

At last Arthur gets the ball again, and actually drives it forward for two, and feels prouder than when he got the three best prizes at hearing Tom's shout of joy, "Well played! well played, young un!"

But the next ball is too much for a young hand, and his bails fly different ways. Nine runs to make and two wickets to go down; it is too much for human nerves.

Before Winter can get in, the omnibus which is to take the M.C.C. men to the train pulls up at the side of the close, and Mr. Aislabie and Tom consult, and give out that the stumps will be drawn after the next over. And so ends the great match. Winter and Johnson carry out their bats, and it being a one day match, the Lord's men are declared the winners, they having scored the most in the first innings.

But such a defeat is a victory; so think Tom and all the School Eleven as they accompany their conquerors to the omnibus and send them off with three ringing cheers, after Mr. Aislabie has shaken hands all round, saying to Tom, "I must compliment you, sir, on your eleven, and I hope we shall have you for a member if you come up to town."

THOMAS HUGHES:
Tom Brown's Schooldays.

Exercises

1. (Boys only.) Explain the cricket terms used in this lesson.
2. What was the result of the match?
3. Describe the picture on page 141.
4. Make sentences containing the following words:

toughest	countenance	deserted
applause	superb	compliment
excitement	spectators	favourite
furious	triumph	astonishment

5. Make a list of twelve more words from the lesson which you find difficult to spell.
6. Give in other words the meaning of each of the following phrases:

like a flash of lightning.
who are now mustering strong.
he feels that a crisis has passed.
to give his men pluck.
working like horses.
holds a short parley with his men.
with a rueful countenance.
the crowd scarcely breathes.
we shall have you for a member.

7. What did Mr. Aislabie mean when he said to Tom, "I must compliment you, sir, on your eleven, and I hope we shall have you for a member if you come up to town"?
8. Can we play cricket in the West Indies at eight o'clock? Why not? How is it they can play in England at that time?

LESSON 26

THE RIVER

Introduction.—Charles Kingsley describes in this poem, with great power and truth, how the nature of a river changes in its course from where it rises "clear and cool" among the hills till, increasing ever as it flows through scenes both lovely and ugly, by fresh meadows and by murky towns, at length it reaches the sea.

CLEAR and cool, clear and cool,
By laughing shallow and dreaming pool;
Cool and clear, cool and clear,
By shining shingle and foaming weir;
Under the crag where the ouzel* sings,
And the ivied wall where the church bell rings,
Undefiled, for the undefiled;
Play by me, bathe in me, mother and child.

Dank and foul, dank and foul,
By the smoky town in its murky cowl;
Foul and dank, foul and dank,
By wharf and sewer and slimy bank;
Darker and darker the farther I go,
Baser and baser the richer I grow;
Who dare sport with the sin-defiled?
Shrink from me, turn from me, mother and child.

Strong and free, strong and free,
The flood-gates are open, away to the sea;
Free and strong, free and strong,
Cleansing my streams as I hurry along

* A small bird.

To the golden sands, and the leaping bar,
And the taintless tide that awaits me afar,
As I lose myself in the infinite main,
Like a soul that has sinned and is pardoned again.
Undefiled, for the undefiled;
Play by me, bathe in me, mother and child.

CHARLES KINGSLEY.

EXERCISES

1. Draw an imaginary map of the river showing where it is (*a*) undefiled, (*b*) dank and foul, (*c*) cleansed.
2. Make sentences containing the following words:
   foaming, weir, ouzel, ivied, undefiled, cowl, wharf,
   slimy, baser, cleansing, taintless, infinite, main.
3. Is the ouzel a West Indian bird?
4. Make a little drawing of a "foaming weir."

LESSON 27

PICTURE LESSONS—VII

BREAD WINNERS

THERE are many ways of earning a living, many different kinds of "breadwinners." Some people earn their daily bread in factories, some in offices, shops, or banks. Some earn it in the country, some on the sea, and some on its shores. On page 149 we see a group of breadwinners who earn it on the shore.

They are carrying something in a sack and in baskets. What do you think the baskets contain? We associate the baskets and the seashore with fishing; so that if we thought that the women had been gathering bait for fishing we should probably not be far wrong.

We can see at a glance that these women are not West Indian or even British folk, as they wear "sabots," or wooden shoes, which are the common footwear of French or Dutch peasants. They are probably helping fathers or brothers, who are fishermen, by gathering the shellfish which are used as bait for the fishing lines. As soon as the tide begins to go out they follow it over the stony and muddy shore, gathering bait for the lines.

In the picture the principal group consists of three women and a baby. The artist has been careful to introduce "variety" into the group. The nearest figure is an old, old woman, with a sack—probably of shellfish—over her shoulder and a basket hanging at her side. The middle woman has taken her baby with her to the shore. Perhaps there was no one to take care of it at home.

The woman to the right is young—little more than a girl—but old enough and strong enough to do her share of the work. We can just see other groups of women at the left side of the picture, but in the distance. As they are small and unimportant they are not so carefully painted as the figures in the foreground. In the background we see the ocean and the sky.

There are no very bright colours in the picture. It may be that the artist wanted to impress us with the monotony of the women's occupation. If he had been painting a picture of children building sand castles on the shore, do you think he would have used such dull colours? And if not, why?

In "Breadwinners" the sky and sea, the shore, and the dresses of the women are all grey; not all the same kind of grey, of course—the painter was too good an artist to

BREADWINNERS.
(Robert M'Gregor, R.S.A., 1847–1922. By kind permission of the Glasgow Art Gallery.)

make his picture dull, even though it was mostly grey. If you look at the picture intelligently you will see warm greys, dull, cold greys, light greys, dark greys, blue greys, and yellow greys.

Here and there in the picture the artist has used some stronger, brighter colours. We notice this especially in the old woman's headdress. The picture is rather roughly painted, and this suits the subject very well.

It appeals to our sympathy. We are made to feel that these are people ministering to other people's comfort who do not get very much comfort for themselves.

LESSON 28

RALEIGH IN TRINIDAD AND GUYANA

TOWARDS the end of the sixteenth century another of the adventurous sons of Devon of whom we read in Lesson 21, Sir Walter Raleigh by name, was dreaming new dreams of empire. In those days the air was full of the rumours of El Dorado, the Golden City, in South America, situated somewhere between the Orinoco and the Amazon, where the streets, it was said, were paved with gold and the pebbles on the pathways were diamonds and pearls. These rumours drew men from their homes to take the chance of life or death in unknown wilds—as gold has ever done and ever will do. The Spaniards themselves had tried in vain to discover the city, but had only succeeded in awakening the hatred of the natives who lived in that region.

To find this Golden City now became the great aim of Raleigh. Having fitted out an expedition at his own expense, he set off in 1595, and called at Trinidad, which, of course, had remained a Spanish possession since its discovery ninety-seven years before. After visiting La Brea, where he caulked his ships with pitch, as we shall learn from his own words on page 187, Raleigh proceeded up the Gulf of Paria to what is now Port of Spain, the capital of Trinidad.

He found deer and wild pigs on the island, and "fruits, fish, and fowls," besides "sufficient maize, cassava, and of the roots and fruits which are common everywhere in the West Indies." He described the soil as excellent, and added that it "will bear sugar, ginger, or any other commodity that the Indies yield."

Raleigh.

At Port of Spain he was visited by some Spaniards whom he entertained and feasted, gathering from them much vague information about Guyana and its riches, particularly the golden-roofed city of Manoa. He also found out from a Carib *cacique* what the strength of the Spanish was, as he was anxious to take revenge on Don Antonio de Berreo, the Governor, for having betrayed eight Englishmen the previous year. His warlike spirit was further roused by hearing of De Berreo's cruelties to the natives.

Accordingly he set upon the guard at daybreak and captured the capital, San José, now the small town of St. Joseph, seven miles from Port of Spain, and took De Berreo and his companions back to the ships in triumph. He then set out on his venture into the unknown, heading for the mouths of the Orinoco, which he explored with the assistance of his prisoner, who was already acquainted with the district. The natives received the strangers with great kindness when they heard they were enemies of Spain; and as they passed along the great river, fringed with giant forests on either side, the hearts of the adventurers beat high with hope.

The legend of El Dorado seems to have been started by one Martinez, a man who, some sixty years before, had been marooned on the Orinoco by the leader of a Spanish expedition. Martinez was afterwards captured by the Indians, and was carried (so he said) to Manoa, to which place he journeyed blindfold in order that he might never be able to betray the position of the Golden City. He avowed at his death that he entered the city at noon, and then uncovered his face, and that he travelled all that day till night through the city, and the next day from sunrise to sunset before he came to the palace of Inga, their chief.

After Martinez had been seven months in Manoa, and began to understand the language of the country, Inga asked him whether he desired to return into his own country or would stay with him. Martinez, like other castaways, pined for home and friends, and had no wish to remain for the rest of his life with any

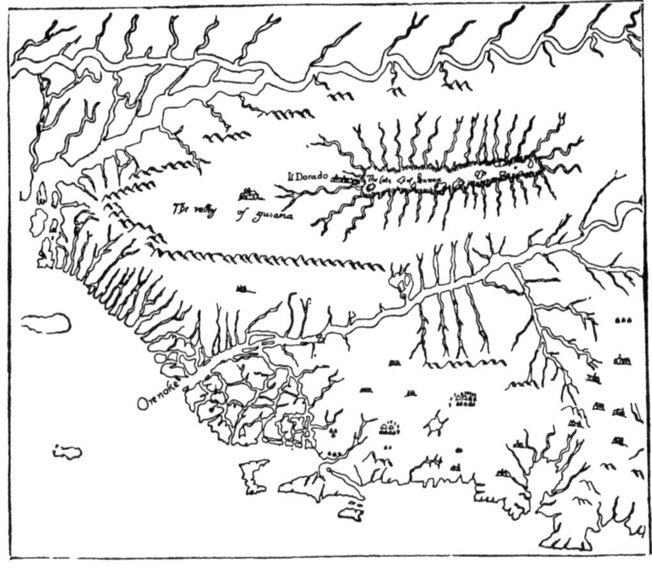

Part of Raleigh's Map of Guyana showing El Dorado.
(Note that the top of the map is the South.)

strange race, so he bargained with Inga that he might depart.

According to his story, the chief sent him away with a party of the Guianese, all laden with as much gold as they could carry, but when they reached the Orinoco the natives there robbed him of all the treasure. It is almost needless to add that he never reached his native land. He died in Puerto Rico while waiting for a passage to Spain, and his knowledge of the road to Manoa passed away with him. He it was who christened the city by the name of El Dorado, from the abundance of gold which he is said to have seen there, the images of gold in their temples, and the plates, armour, and shields of gold which they used in war.

This, then, was the famous city in search of which Sir Walter Raleigh toiled up the Orinoco, suffering many hardships, seeing many strange sights, and hearing of things even more strange, the account of which is to be found in his wonderful story of the *Discoverie of Guiana*.

"I never saw a more beautiful country," he wrote, "nor more lively prospects. . . . All fair, green grass; the deer crossing in every path; the birds towards evening singing on every tree, with a thousand several tunes; cranes and herons of white and crimson perching on the river-side; the air fresh with a gentle easterly wind, *and every stone that we picked up promised either gold or silver by its complexion.*"

His men also brought him "a kind of stone like sapphires; what they might prove to be I know not. I showed them to some of the natives, and they promised to bring me to a mountain that had of them very large pieces growing diamond-wise. Whether it be crystal of the mountain, Bristol diamond, or sapphire, I do not yet know, but I hope the best. Sure I am, that the place is as likely as those from whence all the rich stones are brought."

Speaking of this mountain, he says: "When it grew towards sunset we entered a branch of the river that fell into the Orinoco, where I was informed of the Mountain of Crystal, to which in truth, for the length of the way and the evil season of the year, I was not able to march, nor abide any longer upon the journey: we saw it afar off, and it appeared like a white church tower of exceeding height. . . .

A Ship of the time of Raleigh.

There falleth over it a mighty river. . . . I think there is not in the world so strange an overfall nor so wonderful to behold. . . . Berreo told me that there were diamonds and other precious stones on it, and that they shined very far off: but what it hath I know not."

As he went farther up the river his hopes were raised still higher by meeting with friendly natives, who told him much of Manoa, the El Dorado of his dreams. They were willing, they told him, to take up arms and march against that city, not for its gold, but to take revenge upon its inhabitants, who had ravaged their lands and carried off their women as slaves. But, meantime, it seemed absurd to attack a city, famed for its strength, with a handful of men and a few native tribes. So, leaving one of his men behind in exchange for the son of a native chief, he sailed back to England to ask the government for a strong expedition which he might lead against the City of Gold.

Of the gold mines which Raleigh had hoped to find the seekers discovered no sign, nor has Manoa ever again been looked upon by the eye of a stranger since that day when Martinez, laden with treasure, said farewell to its walls; nor has that "Mountain of Crystal" been found, with its diamonds that "shined very far off." Gold, however, as well as diamonds, has been found of late years in considerable quantities in Guyana, as we learned in Lesson 9, so we are left to wonder how much truth there was in those rumours which so excited the world four hundred years ago.

Exercises

1. What is the difference between "a thousand several tunes" and "several thousand tunes"?
2. How much of the story of Martinez do you think was true?
3. What strange sights did Sir Walter Raleigh see up the Orinoco?
4. What words in the lesson have a similar meaning to each of the following?—

wished	speech	remain
made watertight	left alone	waterfall
produce (*noun*)	named	laid waste
had knowledge of	plenty	reports

5. Imagine yourself to have been cast away upon a desolate island in the Orinoco, captured by Indians, and taken away to the Golden City. Tell your story in your own words.
6. Fill in the blanks:
   (*a*) It was in —— that —— sailed from Plymouth in search of ——, the City of ——, which the —— called El ——.

(*b*) The —— who inhabited this great —— were believed to have been those who had fled from Peru after the Spanish conquest of that ——.

(*c*) Martinez was marooned on the —— about the year ——.

(*d*) Although El —— proved to be but a dream, the voyage was not made in vain, for literature was made —— by Raleigh's book, —— —— ——.

7. What famous waterfall is in Guyana?
8. Why did not Raleigh explore the "Mountain of Crystal"?

LESSON 29

BLACK DOG

Introduction.—In the year 17— there came an old seaman with tarry pigtail and scarred, nut-brown face, across one cheek of which was the scar of a sabre-cut, to the "Admiral Benbow," a lonely inn on the top of some steep cliffs on the western coast of England near Bristol. Few callers visited this isolated spot, which overlooked a little cove where the sea roared in fury on stormy nights.

The "Captain," as he preferred to be called, was an unwelcome visitor, for months passed by and his bill remained unpaid; when he took more rum than was good for him he would sing vile old sea-songs, and tell stories of terrible deeds on the Spanish Main. The innkeeper had fallen sick, and young Jim Hawkins and his mother, the innkeeper's wife, were kept busy.

Though the old sailor was an extremely violent man—on one occasion he was subdued by the village doctor, who threatened to drag him before his Honour at the Sessions—he appeared to be in mortal fear of meeting a man with one leg, and he gave Jim a silver fourpenny piece every month to "keep his weather eye open" for a seafaring man of that description.

It was one January morning, very early—a pinching, frosty morning—the cove all grey with hoar-frost, the ripple lapping softly on the stones, the sun still low and only touching the hill-tops and shining far to seaward. The captain had risen earlier than usual, and set out down the beach, his cutlass swinging under the broad skirts of the old blue coat, his brass telescope under his arm, his hat tilted back upon his head. I remember his breath hanging like smoke in his wake as he strode off, and the last sound I heard of him as he turned the big rock was a loud snort of indignation, as though his mind was still running upon Dr. Livesey.

Well, mother was upstairs with father; and I was laying the breakfast-table against the captain's return, when the parlour door opened, and a man stepped in on whom I had never set my eyes before. He was a pale, tallowy creature, wanting two fingers of the left hand; and though he wore a cutlass, he did not look much like a fighter. I had always my eye open for seafaring men, with one leg or two, and I remember this one puzzled me. He was not sailorly, and yet he had a smack of the sea about him too.

I asked him what was for his service, and he said he would take rum; but as I was going out of the room to fetch it he sat down upon a table and motioned me to draw near. I paused where I was with my napkin in my hand.

"Come here, sonny," says he. "Come nearer here."

I took a step nearer.

"Is this here table for my mate Bill?" he asked, with a kind of leer.

I told him I did not know his mate Bill; and this was for a person who stayed in our house, whom we called the captain.

"Well," he said, "my mate Bill would be called the captain, as like as not. He has a cut on one cheek, and a mighty pleasant way with him, particularly in drink, has my mate Bill. We'll put it, for argument like, that your captain has a cut on one cheek—and we'll put it, if you like, that that cheek's the right one. Ah, well! I told you. Now, is my mate Bill in this here house?"

I told him he was out walking.

"Which way, sonny? Which way is he gone?"

And when I had pointed out the rock and told him how the captain was likely to return, and how soon, and answered a few other questions, "Ah," said he, "this'll be as good as drink to my mate Bill."

The expression of his face as he said these words was not at all pleasant, and I had my own reasons for thinking that the stranger was mistaken, even supposing he meant what he said. But it was no affair of mine, I thought; and besides, it was difficult to know what to do. The stranger kept hanging about just inside the inn door, peering round the corner like a cat waiting for a mouse. Once I stepped out myself into the road, but he immediately called me back, and as I did not obey quick enough for his fancy, a most horrible change came over his tallowy face, and he ordered me in, with an oath that made me jump. As soon as I was back again he returned to his former manner, half fawning, half sneering, patted me on the shoulder, told me I was a good boy, and he had taken quite a fancy to me. "I have a son of my own," said he, "as like you as two blocks, and he's all the pride of my 'art. But the great thing for boys is discipline, sonny—discipline. Now, if you had sailed along of

Bill, you wouldn't have stood there to be spoke to twice—not you. That was never Bill's way, nor the way of sich as sailed with him. And here, sure enough, is my mate Bill, with a spy-glass under his arm, bless his old 'art, to be sure. You and me'll just go back into the parlour, sonny, and get behind the door, and we'll give Bill a little surprise—bless his 'art, I say again."

So saying, the stranger backed along with me into the parlour, and put me behind him in the corner, so that we were both hidden by the open door. I was very uneasy and alarmed, as you may fancy, and it rather added to my fears to observe that the stranger was certainly frightened himself. He cleared the hilt of his cutlass and loosened the blade in the sheath; and all the time we were waiting there he kept swallowing as if he felt what we used to call a lump in the throat.

At last in strode the captain, slammed the door behind him, without looking to the right or left, and marched straight across the room to where his breakfast awaited him.

"Bill," said the stranger, in a voice that I thought he had tried to make bold and big.

The captain spun round on his heel and fronted us; all the brown had gone out of his face, and even his nose was blue; he had the look of a man who sees a ghost, or the Evil One, or something worse, if anything can be; and, upon my word, I felt sorry to see him, all in a moment, turn so old and sick.

"Come, Bill, you know me; you know an old shipmate, Bill, surely," said the stranger.

The captain made a sort of gasp.

"Black Dog!" said he.

"And who else?" returned the other, getting more at his ease. "Black Dog as ever was, come for to see his old shipmate Billy, at the 'Admiral Benbow' inn. Ah, Bill, Bill, we have seen a sight of times, us two, since I lost them two talons," holding up his mutilated hand.

"Now, look here," said the captain; "you've run me down; here I am; well, then, speak up: what is it?"

"That's you, Bill," returned Black Dog, "you're in the right of it, Billy. I'll have a glass of rum from this dear child here, as I've took such a liking to; and we'll sit down, if you please, and talk square, like old shipmates."

When I returned with the rum, they were already seated on either side of the captain's breakfast-table—Black Dog next to the door, and sitting sideways, so as to have one eye on his old shipmate, and one, as I thought, on his retreat.

He bade me go, and leave the door wide open. "None of your keyholes for me, sonny," he said; and I left them together, and retired into the bar.

For a long time, though I certainly did my best to listen, I could hear nothing but a low gabbling; but at last the voices began to grow higher, and I could pick up a word or two, mostly oaths, from the captain.

"No, no, no, no; and an end of it!" he cried once. And again, "If it comes to swinging, swing all, say I."

Then all of a sudden there was a tremendous explosion of oaths and other noises—the chair and table went over in a lump, a clash of steel followed, and then a cry of pain, and the next instant I saw Black Dog in full flight, and the captain hotly pursuing, both with drawn cutlasses, and the former streaming blood from the left shoulder. Just at the door the captain aimed at the fugitive one last tremendous cut, which would certainly have split him to the chine had it not been intercepted by our big signboard of Admiral Benbow. You may see the notch on the lower side of the frame to this day.

That blow was the last of the battle. Once out upon the road, Black Dog, in spite of his wound, showed a wonderful clean pair of heels, and disappeared over the edge of the hill in half a minute. The captain, for his part, stood staring at the signboard like a bewildered man. Then he passed his hand over his eyes several times, and at last turned back into the house.

"Jim," says he, "rum;" and as he spoke he reeled a little, and caught himself with one hand against the wall.

"Are you hurt?" cried I.

"Rum," he repeated. "I must get away from here. Rum! rum!"

I ran to fetch it; but I was quite unsteadied by all that had fallen out, and I broke one glass and fouled the tap, and while I was still getting in my own way I heard a loud fall in the parlour, and running in, beheld the captain lying full length upon the floor. At the same instant my mother, alarmed by the cries and fighting, came running downstairs to help me. Between us we raised his head. He was breathing very loud and hard; but his eyes were closed, and his face a horrible colour.

"Dear, deary me," cried my mother, "what a disgrace upon the house! And your poor father sick!"

In the meantime we had no idea what to do to help the captain, nor any other thought but that he had got his death-hurt in the scuffle with the stranger. I got the rum, to be sure, and tried to put it down his throat; but his teeth were tightly shut, and his jaws as strong as iron. It was a happy relief for us when the door opened and Doctor Livesey came in, on his visit to my father.

"Oh, doctor," we cried, "what shall we do? Where is he wounded?"

"Wounded! A fiddlestick's end!" said the doctor. "No more wounded than you or I. The man has had a stroke, as I warned him. Now, Mrs. Hawkins, just you run upstairs to your husband, and tell him, if possible, nothing about it. For my part, I must do my best to save this fellow's trebly worthless life; and Jim here will get me a basin."

When I got back with the basin, the doctor had already ripped up the captain's sleeve and exposed his great sinewy arm. It was tattooed in several places. "Here's luck," "A fair wind," and "Billy Bones his fancy," were very neatly and clearly executed on the forearm; and up near the shoulder there was a sketch of a gallows and a man hanging from it—done, as I thought, with great spirit.

"Prophetic," said the doctor, touching this picture with his finger. "And now, Master Billy Bones, if that be your name, we'll have a look at the colour of your blood. Jim," he said, "are you afraid of blood?"

"No, sir," said I.

"Well, then," said he, "you hold the basin;" and with that he took his lancet and opened a vein.

A great deal of blood was taken before the captain opened his eyes and looked mistily about him. First he recognized the doctor with an unmistakable frown; then his glance fell upon me, and he looked relieved. But suddenly his colour changed, and he tried to raise himself, crying—

"Where's Black Dog?"

"There is no Black Dog here," said the doctor, "except what you have on your own back. You have been drinking rum; you have had a stroke, precisely as I told you; and I have just, very much against my own will, dragged you head-foremost out of the grave. Now, Mr. Bones——"

"That's not my name," he interrupted.

"Much I care," returned the doctor. "It's the name of a buccaneer of my acquaintance; and I call you by it for the sake of shortness, and what I have to say to you is this: one glass of rum won't kill you, but if you take one you'll take another and another, and I stake my wig if you don't break off short, you'll die—do you understand that?—die, and go to your own place, like the man in the Bible. Come, now, make an effort. I'll help you to your bed for once."

Between us, with much trouble, we managed to hoist him upstairs, and laid him on his bed, where his head fell back on the pillow, as if he were almost fainting.

"Now, mind you," said the doctor, "I clear my conscience—the name of rum for you is death."

And with that he went off to see my father, taking me with him by the arm.

"This is nothing," he said, as soon as he had closed the door. "I have drawn blood enough to keep him quiet a while; he should lie for a week where he is—that is the best thing for him and you; but another stroke would settle him."

R. L. STEVENSON:
Treasure Island.

EXERCISES

1. Describe the lodger at the "Admiral Benbow" and his mode of living.
2. Find some good word-pictures in this story.
3. What is a "tallowy creature"?
4. What is the missing letter in each of these words?—

fu*itive	Jan*ary	oc*asion	cre*ture
o*ths	vi*lent	tel*scope	arg*ment
slam*ed	g*ost	mut*lated	lis*en
inter*epted	no*ch	bas*n	sinew*

5. Give an account of the coming and the going of Black Dog.
6. What effect did his visit have on "the captain"?
7. If you were to visit the "Admiral Benbow," and saw the notch on the signboard, what would it recall?
8. Would you call this a dull or an exciting story?
   Do you want to read more of it?
   It tells of an eventful hunt for treasure.
   The Parts of the Book are called:
   (1) The Old Buccaneer.
   (2) The Sea Cook.
   (3) My Shore Adventure.
   (4) The Stockade.
   (5) My Sea Adventure.
   (6) Captain Silver (Long John).
   Do these headings "whet your appetite"?
   If the book is in your school library you should read it.
9. What did the doctor mean when he touched the tattooed picture on the man's arm and said "Prophetic"?

LESSON 30

PICTURE LESSONS—VIII

A Dutch Landscape

The Dutch painters were the first to paint landscape for its own sake. That is, they were the first artists to paint country scenes in which figures of human beings did not play a prominent part.

While it is quite true that there are at least seven figures in the "Avenue" picture by Hobbema on page 168, they are so small, and so unimportant, that we do not notice them at first.

At the right is a gardener at work, not far from the house there are two people, on the road is a traveller with a dog, and at the far end of the avenue there are several other people. But all of them together do not occupy much space, and do not distract our eyes from the beautiful country scene.

No, what attracts us is the feeling of being out of doors. We can easily imagine ourselves enjoying the golden afternoon sunshine in the flat Dutch country. This is just what Hobbema meant us to do.

When we begin to look at the details of the picture we notice first the double line of trees stretching from the foreground into the extreme distance. At first sight we may think them rather formal and toy-like, resembling the palms of our own country. Such trees are quite common in flat countries like Holland.

The artist might have been tempted to make the trees very like each other, but we notice that each one has a special character and shape of its own! Nature never repeats herself. No two leaves are exactly alike, much less two trees.

The picture pleases us because, when we examine it in detail, we see that, like Nature, it is full of variety. In all the fields, bushes, hedges, buildings, and clouds the same size or shape is never repeated.

Yet the picture, as a whole, is very well balanced, though it is made up of so many varied parts. How naturally the sunshine strikes on the tree trunks, on the edges of the foliage and clouds! What a lovely, quiet blue the sky is!

Now consider again the figures of men and women. Though we have agreed that they are not the chief feature of the picture, they have an important duty to perform—or, rather, a double duty.

They help us to realize, by comparison, the size of other things in the picture, and they give a warm, human feeling to the landscape; for they, like the artist and the spectator, are enjoying the warm, sunny afternoon.

Very little is known of the life of Hobbema. We know from looking at his pictures that he spent his life transferring to canvas with loving care his own beautiful country-side.

He lived and died a poor man, and was buried in a pauper's grave. Though he was a poor man he was not a *poor* painter, and has gained immortality by his glorious landscapes. "The Avenue, Middelharnis," hangs in the National Gallery in London, and it is his masterpiece.

THE AVENUE, MIDDELHARNIS, HOLLAND.
(*Meyndert Hobbema. 1638–1709. The National Gallery, London.*)

LESSON 31

WATER

WATER, like air, is a prime necessity of life. None of the different parts of our bodies can live and work without it; even bone, which seems so hard and dry, is kept alive by water. On the other hand, water may be a source of danger to life, as it is a means whereby many harmful things may be introduced into the body.

Water is essential not only as an article of diet, but also for the cleanliness of our bodies, clothes, and houses, for trade and manufacturing purposes, and for protection against fire. For these reasons people in early times nearly always built their settlements on or near to the banks of rivers, which also served as roads.

Water may exist in three forms: Under ordinary conditions it is the clear tasteless fluid that we know as rain or river water; if cooled to a low temperature it becomes solid—it freezes—and is known as ice; if heated to a high temperature it is changed into a gas or vapour.

The importance of water to our bodies cannot be exaggerated. It enters into the composition of our tissues, forming about 70 per cent of the entire body weight. Our food must be in a fluid state in order to penetrate into our tissues, and the waste products of our bodies are also given off mainly in solution.

Our bodies require about *three pints* of water daily, and the neglect to drink sufficient water is a very general fault; but the mistake of drinking too much water at meals should not be made, as water cannot take the place of thorough mastication.

It is generally stated that water is obtained from the following different sources: rain, streams or rivers, ponds, lakes, and wells; but in reality all these are parts of a vast system of circulation.

All water apparently comes to us as rain, but it starts in an earlier stage as water vapour which was evaporated or distilled by the action of the sun from the collections of

water on the earth, such as seas, rivers, and lakes. This vapour rises up into the colder atmosphere, where it forms clouds, condenses into a liquid, and falls to the earth as rain. It sometimes falls as a solid in the form of hail or small lumps of ice, after it has passed through a *very* cold region and become frozen. In some countries it also falls as snow, a white feather-like substance which is also frozen rain; but we do not see this in the tropics. There is thus a continuous circle or cycle going on—water, evaporation, cloud, rain, and then water again.

When water falls as rain it is distributed in various ways: some of it is evaporated; a part of it sinks into the ground; the rest of it flows off in the direction of the slope of the land to join streams, rivers, lakes, and ponds. Rain water thus becomes "surface water," and after penetrating into the ground this takes the form of "ground water," and is again available in wells, or may reappear at the surface as "springs."

You can see from the diagram on the opposite page how water circulates, and the diagram on this page shows

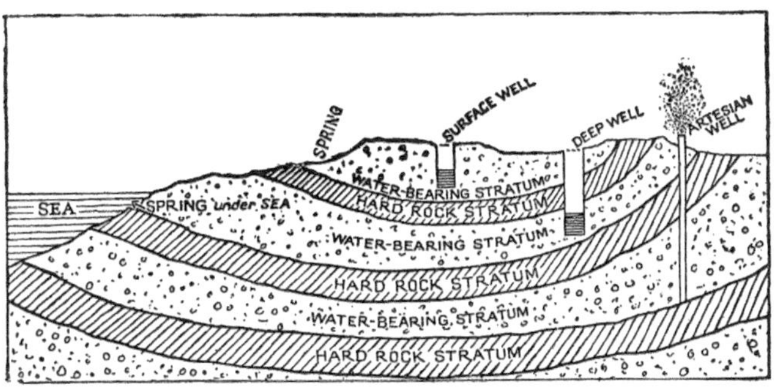

how the distribution of water takes place. That which soaks through the ground eventually reaches a layer of the earth's crust, such as hard rock or clay, which does not let it pass through readily. It then flows on until it may appear at the surface as a spring. You can also see that the water which collects in "surface" or shallow wells only passes through the first water-bearing stratum or layer of the earth, whereas that of "deep" wells passes down to the next stratum through a thickness of filtering soil as well as the first hard layer.

It is thus easy to realize that water from these various sources must vary in purity. The impurities which may be present are numerous: dust blows in, taking disease germs and the eggs and young of parasites of various kinds; sewage soaks through the soil; dirty water from roofs enters tanks; decaying parts of plants or animals, small living creatures of various kinds, metals such as lead, or substances such as sulphur, may be present and injurious. Good water fit to drink should contain none of these impurities.

Rain water is distilled water—that is, water which has been vaporized and condensed—and as it leaves the clouds it is the purest form of water in Nature. It readily takes up impurities, however, from the atmosphere through which it falls, and from the roofs and other surfaces from which it is collected. Care must be taken to keep the tanks, vats, or cisterns in which it is stored clean and free from mosquito larvæ. These receptacles should be made of concrete if possible, or be cement lined, and the water should pass through strong wire-gauze strainers to prevent dead leaves, dust, dead locusts, bats, lizards, and the excrement of birds or other creatures being washed into them, or mosquitoes entering to deposit their eggs. An even better method is to pass the water through a filter of small stone and sand, which will remove small particles of impurities that could pass through the meshes of the gauze.

Rivers and streams run along the natural drainage lines of the country, and so are liable to receive waste and washings from the surrounding area. Shallow wells, therefore, require protection from such surface washings and drainage. You can see from the diagram that such wells are also liable to be polluted by drainage from a considerable distance, as impurities may soak through the soil and find their way into the wells.

All wells should have a perfect cover, and within a certain distance round them no animal should be admitted, no slop-water, filth, rubbish, or fluid of any kind be allowed to be thrown, and no excrement of any kind permitted to be deposited. People should not wash themselves or their clothing near a well.

The water of deep wells is generally pure, as it has passed through a filtering layer of hard soil, but it frequently contains so much mineral matter as to be unsuitable for such domestic purposes as the washing of clothes.

Water supplies, except those taken from uninhabited and uncultivated regions and from deep wells, are thus liable to contain substances which may be injurious to health. The greatest risk is that arising from contamination by the waste matter from houses, as this may contain the germs of diseases such as typhoid fever, dysentery, and diarrhœa.

Protection of drinking-water from such contamination is a duty we owe to ourselves and our neighbours. If we neglect this duty serious consequences may result.

Where large quantities of water have to be collected for the supply of a town or large village it is difficult to prevent pollution. Methods of purification, such as filtering through sand or treatment by chemical substances, are frequently adopted.

Despite all the possibilities of impurities being present, there is one easy and effective precaution that can be taken in any house to make the water fit for human use, and that is to boil the drinking-water and keep it at the boil for a few minutes. This kills the disease germs and the eggs of all parasites.

Boiled water has a flat taste on account of the air having been driven out by boiling, but if allowed to stand for some time it again absorbs air and loses this unpleasant quality.

Exercises

1. Give the plural form of each of the following:

myself	stratum	larva
mosquito	radius	deer

2. There are many words in this lesson which are never, or very seldom, used in the plural, such as *health, atmosphere, evaporation*. Make a list of such words, and try to discover why they have no plural.
3. Make a list of all the words in this lesson which mean processes. Commence with *cooled, heated,* etc.
4. Explain the difference between a *shallow* and a *deep* well. Illustrate your answer by a drawing.
5. How is a spring formed?
6. Which sources of water are likely to be pure and which impure? Give reasons in each case.
7. In many large towns pure water can be obtained either from pipes inside the houses or from standpipes in the streets. Where was this water collected? What steps have been taken to make it pure?
8. What diseases can be contracted by drinking impure water? What steps can you take to (*a*) ensure that your drinking water is pure, and (*b*) protect the source of supply from contamination?
9. "Water is a prime necessity of life." Explain what is meant by this.

LESSON 32

BRITAIN GAINS A FOOTHOLD IN THE WEST INDIES

WE have seen how Columbus was the first to claim territory in the West Indies in the name of the King of Spain. For many years after their discovery the islands remained in the possession of Spain, but the Spaniards, in their eagerness for gold, cared little for the rich vegetable products of the islands, and left the smaller ones, such as Barbados and St. Kitts, practically untouched.

The first English settlement was made in the latter island in 1623 under Captain Thomas Warner. He was soon joined by a French privateering party, who were welcomed by the English, as they were expecting an attack by the warlike Caribs. The English and French together drove out the natives and divided the land between them, holding it till they were themselves dislodged by a Spanish fleet later on. They then fled to several of the neighbouring islands of the Windward and Leeward groups, which at first were merely pirate strongholds, but became in after-days permanent settlements. In this irregular fashion the British gained their first foothold in the West Indies. As the greater number of the Lesser Antilles were thus settled by the English from St. Kitts, this island has been called "The Mother of the Antilles."

The first real colony planted here, however, was that of Barbados in 1626. A ship belonging to a certain rich London merchant on its way home from South America was driven by a storm into the harbour of that island, and the sailors were astonished to find on the shore a cross bearing an inscription to the effect that in 1605 the captain of the good ship *Orange Blossom* had taken possession of the island in the name of King James the First of England. They carried home such an account of the beauty and fertility of the place that two vessels, containing about forty emigrants, were sent out by this merchant, Sir William Courteen. They landed on the leeward side of the island, and began to build a city, which they loyally called Jamestown, after their king.

Their captain then proceeded to Essequibo in Guyana where he obtained from a Dutchman seeds and plants of cassava, yams, Indian corn, sweet potatoes, plantains, oranges, limes, pineapples, sugar cane, tobacco, cotton and annatto, with which he returned to Barbados. He also took back with him a Carib to show the settlers how the plants should be cultivated.

Three years later another party arrived and founded on Carlisle Bay a town named Bridgetown from a bridge which they built across the stream there. Immediately a jealous rivalry arose between the two parties that led to bloodshed for a while, until a third band under a governor appeared on the scene and order was restored. The island then began to flourish exceedingly, and has continued to do so ever since. Barbados has a unique record among the important islands of the British West Indies, in that it was originally settled by the British and remained British until 1966.

For the largest British island, Jamaica, however, we had to fight with Spain. Several raids had been made on the island by the adventurous buccaneers over a space of fifty years or more, but it was not until 1654 that any organized expedition left England with the object of wresting from Spain some of her West Indian possessions. Towards the end of that year a fleet of thirty-eight ships, under Admiral Sir William Penn, having on board a force of about three thousand soldiers under the command of General Venables, sailed for the West Indies to capture Hispaniola.

Oliver Cromwell was at that time Lord Protector of England, and the force given to Penn and Venables, who were both suspected of being "King's men," was "a sad mixture of distempered, unruly persons"—royalist soldiers for the most part, who had no heart to serve under Cromwell's leaders. The results were as unsatisfactory as the quality of the troops.

Their attempt to take Hispaniola ended in disaster. The men behaved shamefully, and they suffered severe losses at the hands of the Spanish. Penn and Venables, dreading the disgrace of returning home defeated, decided to retrieve their honour by taking another Spanish island. On the 9th of May Jamaica was sighted, its towering mountains half hidden in the morning mist. Here another attempt was to be made to carry out Cromwell's instructions.

But Penn did not care this time to trust entirely to the land force. The fleet ran in and anchored near what was later called Port Royal, the little *Martin,* a twelve-gun galley, engaging a Spanish fort at the water's edge. In this instance the Spaniards behaved as feebly as our men had done at Hispaniola. No sooner were the boats containing the landing-party seen to leave the ships than the garrison abandoned their guns and fled towards the town to join their main body. There was no fighting, no glory gleaned for either side; the Spaniards yielded, tamely surrendering to Venables.

The fact was that owing to the mismanagement of Spain, the population of the island had dwindled away, until it consisted only of some scattered and quarrelsome remnants of old Spanish families, and a large number of negro slaves brought over from Africa.

England therefore gained a magnificent island, after Cuba and Hispaniola the largest in the West Indies, although the Spaniards had left in it as little as possible. When Venables, at the head of his rabble, marched into the town of St. Jago, there was little found but the bare walls—everything portable had been carried off, to the bitter disappointment of the soldiers. In their search for hidden treasure, houses were destroyed, the abbey and churches demolished, and the very church bells melted down.

Long afterwards large quantities of ancient copper coins were unearthed in the hills around St. Jago, but no other treasure has ever been found. The Spaniards had carried off with them to Cuba their gold and silver, and had buried the bulkier and less valuable copper.

At first the progress of the island was very slow. Cromwell, who seems to have taken a great interest in this his one foreign conquest, was very anxious to transport thither the whole of the Puritan settlers from New England in North America; but the stern sons of the Pilgrim Fathers had grown to love their bracing seaboard, and would not hear of exchanging it even for the fertile charms of Jamaica.

THE BRITISH UNDER ADMIRAL PENN AND GENERAL VENABLES ENTERING KINGSTON HARBOUR.
(*From a drawing by R. Caton Woodville, R.I.*)

Numbers of Irish and Scots were then sent out as settlers, but disease broke out and many of them died. They also suffered much from the attacks of the "Maroons"—the negroes whom the Spaniards had brought into the island, and who were now living as outlaws in the mountains. Eventually prosperity began to appear. The land was rich; there was useful work to be done if there were the right men to do it. Things began to mend after the importation of African slaves, so that out of evil came much good.

In 1658 Spain made an attempt to regain her lost territory, and her troops were actually in the island for some time before the officer in command of the English forces, General Doyley, had any knowledge of their presence. They were soon defeated, however, and Jamaica has since remained a British colony. Gradually the fertile soil was laid out into plantations, and towns began to arise; but for many years the chief riches of the island were drawn from the exploits of the buccaneers, who made Jamaica their headquarters, as we shall see in another lesson.

Exercises

1. What is the difference between "the ships' sides" and "the ship's sides"?
2. Of what fact are Barbadians naturally very proud?
3. Which island is fairly entitled to be called the Mother Colony of the West Indies? Why?
4. What sort of force was under the command of Venables? Say how it acquitted itself in the engagements in which it took part?
5. Why did the Spaniards bury their copper? Where did they go when they left Jamaica? Why did they go there? What did they take with them?
6. If in 1658 Britain could be said to have secured a firm foothold for both feet, in which islands would her two feet be placed?

7. Study the picture on page 179. What things can you see which differ much from those of the present day?
8. Fill in the blanks in the following passages:
   (*a*) The first British settlement was in St. Kitts in ——, whereas —— was settled three years later in 1626.
   (*b*) —— has the distinction of being the only —— island in the West Indies over which no foreign —— has ever flown.
   (*c*) The Cayman —— were taken possession of by the English soon after the conquest of the neighbouring island of ——, the largest of the British West ——. They were mainly colonized from that ——.
   (*d*) By a treaty concluded at ——, the capital of Spain, in 1670, the possession of Jamaica and the other —— —— islands, then held by her, was confirmed to England.
   (*e*) Jamaica has had to contend with natural forces in her history. In 1692 Port —— was destroyed by an —— that hurled whole streets of houses into the sea. The next year, as the walls of the —— were slowly —— once again, a —— arose which swept them completely away.

LESSON 33

THE GLOVE AND THE LIONS

KING FRANCIS* was a hearty king, and loved a royal sport;
And one day, as his lions fought, sat looking on the court.
The nobles filled the benches, and the ladies in their pride,
And amongst them sat the Count de Lorge, with one for whom he sighed.

* Francis I. of France. He was a brave and warlike king, fond of display. He met Henry VIII. of England near Calais on what was called "The Field of the Cloth of Gold" from the magnificence of the camps of the two kings.

And truly 'twas a gallant thing to see that crowning show—Valour and love, and a king above, and the royal beasts below.

Ramped and roared the lions, with horrid, laughing jaws;
They bit, they glared, gave blows like beams, a wind went with their paws;
With wallowing might and stifled roar they rolled on one another,
Till all the pit, with sand and mane, was in a thunderous smother.
The bloody foam above the bars came whisking through the air;
Said Francis then, "Faith, gentlemen, we're better here than there!"

De Lorge's love o'erheard the king—a beauteous, lively dame,
With smiling lips, and sharp, bright eyes, which always seemed the same.
She thought, "The count my lover is as brave as brave can be:
He surely would do wondrous things to show his love for me.
King, ladies, lovers, all look on; the occasion is divine!
I'll drop my glove to prove his love; great glory will be mine!"

She dropped her glove to prove his love, then looked at him and smiled;
He bowed, and in a moment leaped among the lions wild.
The leap was quick, return was quick—he had regained his place;
Then threw the glove, but not with love, right in the lady's face!
"By Heaven!" said Francis, "rightly done!" and he rose from where he sat.
"Not love," quoth he, "but vanity, sets love a task like that."

LEIGH HUNT.

Exercises

1. How many people are mentioned in this poem? Name them.
2. Give a short description in your own words of the scene where this incident took place.
3. Make a list of all the words which tell of the actions of the lions.
4. Why did the lady take this opportunity to prove the love of the count?
5. How did the count know she desired him to regain the glove?
6. Why did the count throw the glove in her face?
7. What was the pit?
8. How do you know the lady was proud of her beauty?
9. Was the king glad or angry when the count threw the glove at the lady? How do you know?
10. Which two of these words have a similar meaning?—
    ramped, roared, stifled, gallant, smothered, whisking, beauteous.

LESSON 34

PICTURE LESSONS—IX

Portrait of an Old Lady

Rembrandt was one of the most famous of the world's painters. Not only was he a great portrait painter, but he was also a painter of Bible pictures, landscapes, and story pictures, as well as a great draughtsman and etcher.

Though he studied for three years under another artist he was practically self-taught. He looked at Nature in his own way, and invented his own painting methods.

When he was painting a portrait he studied the features of his sitters very carefully, and painted in a simple manner exactly what he saw.

This may be seen in the "Portrait of an Old Lady". There she is, exactly as she appeared to Rembrandt about three hundred years ago.

We feel sure that the portrait is not a flattering, but a true likeness. He has not omitted any of her wrinkles, and has noticed and shown us the differences between the right and left sides of her face. We can quite easily test this.

If we compare her two eyes, we will notice that her right one is at a different angle from her left, besides being darker. This sometimes happens in the faces of old people, and Rembrandt's keen eye and deft hand have shown it to us.

PORTRAIT OF AN OLD LADY.
(*Rembrandt, 1606–69.*)

The wrinkle at the right side of her nose is also much deeper and more pronounced than the one at the left side. Do you think the artist would have shown these differences if his eye had not noticed them?

A flattering portrait painter would probably have tried to please the old lady by painting her, not as she was, but as she might have liked to appear.

In this picture we notice that the light comes from the left side (of the spectator), and yet the edge of the shadowed side of her face is very light. This is because "reflected" light comes from the very broad white muslin ruff which encircles her neck.

How gauzy is the muslin of her cap! In the original painting in the National Gallery in London we can even see the heads of the pins which keep it in place. How wonderfully every feature has been modelled!

We may ask why the artist has not shown more detail in the old lady's bodice. It is probable that he wanted to direct our attention specially to her head and face, and that he thought it would distract our attention if he gave the same emphasis to her dress.

Why do you think he has made the upper part of the background darker than the lower?

In the original painting we can just see the figures "83" (the old lady's age) on the light background to the left, and "Rembrandt, 1634" (the year when the portrait was painted), to the right of the picture.

Rembrandt painted more than seven hundred pictures, at least fifty of which were portraits of himself painted by the aid of a mirror. This shows not his vanity, but his industry.

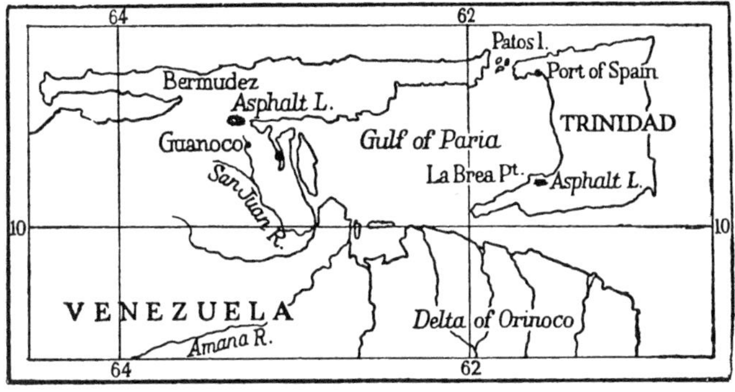

The Asphalt Lakes of Trinidad and Venezuela.

LESSON 35

THE WONDER LAKE IN TRINIDAD

THE West Indies and neighbouring British colonies contain many wonderful and interesting things which are a never-failing attraction to visitors, but the Pitch Lake of Trinidad, one of the natural wonders of the world, possesses strong claims to first place. Its fame has been world-wide since the time of Sir Walter Raleigh, who wrote in his *History of the Discoverie of Guiana:* "From thence I rowed to another port, called by the naturals Piche, and by the Spaniards Tierra de Brea. At this point there is that abundance of stone pitch, that all the shippes of the world may be therewith loden from thence, and we made trial of it in trimming our shippes to be most excellent good, and melteth not with the Sunne as the pitch of Norway, and therefore for shippes trading the south parts very profitable."

The famous lake is situated at La Brea on the Gulf of Paria, in the south-western part of Trinidad, about twelve miles by sea from San Fernando, the second town of the island. It lies in a bowl-like depression about 115 feet above sea-level, and resembles a vast basin of asphalt, around the margin of which is a thin fringe of tropical vegetation.

In appearance the surface is merely an expanse of uninteresting-looking black pitch, which in places rises in gentle mound-shaped masses, around which channels of rain-water trickle. Except for the grasses and weeds on the small "islands," as the various oases in this desert of pitch are called, the only signs of life on its surface are the labourers at work, busily digging the asphalt with their pickaxes and loading it into buckets on the tramway.

The area of the lake is not extensive, being approximately ninety-five acres, but it has yielded up nearly five million tons of pitch without lowering the surface more than about twenty feet. It was long thought to be of unknown depth. Recently, however, soundings have been made by engineers and geologists which have shown that the greatest depth is 285 feet in the centre of the lake, and that the asphalt at all depths is uniform in quality and texture. Thus no one now living will ever see the day when its contents will be exhausted.

One can wander over the surface in perfect safety, for there is only one really soft spot where it is unwise to stand too long. This particular area is known as the "Mother of the Lake," and any object may sink into the asphalt there.

A WAGON ON THE PITCH LAKE.

In spite of this apparent solidity, the pitch is really liquid and is constantly in motion; every hole that is dug fills up slowly just as the surface of water becomes level after it has been disturbed. This internal motion sometimes produces curious effects; pieces of tree trunks are brought up to the surface, and emerge ghost-like to survey the scene for a brief spell, only to disappear once more into the depths beneath. Some years ago, when drilling operations were in progress, the tubes became twisted, broken, and lost in the asphalt; but over a year afterwards the fragments were found reappearing at the surface in entirely different parts of the lake.

Tools for digging pitch.

Although not strictly solid, the pitch is stiff enough to be dug out readily in big lumps with pickaxes. The picture on page 190 gives you a very good idea of this operation. You can also see from it that the crude pitch is sponge-like in appearance. In colour it is a brownish-black, and in this form it contains impurities such as water, finely-powdered clay, sticks, roots, mud, and other matter.

The lumps of pitch are transported from various parts of the lake to the refinery by means of wagons hauled by cable over a light railway, the supporting sleepers of which are moved from time to time as they slowly sink into the surface. The process of refining consists mainly of heating the crude substance in tanks made hot by steam passing through coiled pipes. This has the effect of melting the pitch, driving off water, and removing all other matter except the finely-powdered clay.

The Cable Way to the pier.

The refined pitch, or "dried asphalt," is then run into barrels, where it hardens before being shipped to all parts of the world. A considerable quantity is also

Loading pitch on the lake.

exported in the crude state; in this form it is transported direct from the lake by the cable railway to the weighing station. The buckets are then lifted to an overhead cable tramway supported by towers, and in a long continuous stream they move steadily down the hill and along the pier jutting out into the water, a total distance of a mile, until they reach the vessel waiting to be loaded. The empty buckets then return over the cableway to renew their load.

The greater part of the output is, however, shipped in the refined state, and in this case the buckets are replaced by "skips," each carrying two barrels. By this means eighty tons of crude pitch, or 360 barrels, can be loaded on a ship in an hour.

Trinidad asphalt is now exported to the British Isles and the United States, where many thousands of miles of modern roadway have been constructed with

This photograph shows the consistency of the natural asphalt.

its aid, as well as to many of the leading countries of Europe, South America, Australasia, Asia, and Africa. It has been largely used to restore the roads in the districts of France which were wrecked in the Great War.

The "Land of the Humming-bird" is indeed fortunate in possessing such a valuable natural asset as this "wonder lake." It is a constant source of income to the Government of the colony, as the duty paid on the asphalt exported amounts to about $440,000 per annum. The industry also gives employment to about 1,500 labourers, who are housed in a model village—"New Jersey," in the neighbourhood of the lake—with piped water supply, sewerage, and electric lighting.

It is not generally known that there is a sister lake on the mainland in Venezuela across the Gulf of Paria. The Bermudez Lake, as it is called, is not so easily reached by visitors, and very few tourists have ever seen it. In size it is about ten times as large as its neighbour in Trinidad, but the latter is of far greater depth and produces more asphalt.

The Venezuelan product varies from almost a liquid which oozes up through the water and can be pulled up like seaweed, to a pitch so hard that it can only be removed by blasting. The amount of water on the lake is sometimes very great, and the men engaged in digging are often almost up to their waists in water.

The lake is situated seven miles from the steamer wharf at Guanoco, whither the pitch is transported by a narrow-gauge railway owned by the company which operates both this and the Trinidad lake. The map on page 187 shows the location of the two lakes.

Exercises

1. The quotation in paragraph 1 is given in Raleigh's own spelling. What words do you notice have changed in spelling during the last four hundred years?
2. What is the singular form of "oases"?
3. Is the pitch solid or liquid? How do we know? Do you know of any other substance which resembles it in this way?
4. In what ways is the Pitch Lake of value to Trinidad?
5. Where is there another pitch lake? Draw the sketch map on page 187.
6. Describe the scene shown in the picture on page 189.
7. What happens to the pitch after it leaves the lake before it is exported?
8. Make a list of the twelve words in this lesson which cause you the most difficulty to spell. Learn them thoroughly.
9. Make sentences of your own containing these words:

natural	geologists	fragments	replaced
depression	apparent	operations	tourists
extensive	survey	continuous	gauge

LESSON 36

SOME FRIENDS OF PLANTS

MANY people think that all kinds of insects are harmful, just as many also regard all snakes as poisonous. How often we see men who own guns destroy birds too, without thought as to whether they are useful or harmful! In like manner insects are often destroyed in gardens without any consideration as to whether they do harm or good.

It is true that much damage is caused to stored grain by weevils, and that some insects and birds do much harm to growing crops in the field. This, however, you will learn about in the next book. In this lesson we will consider chiefly those which are of assistance to us in various ways.

Three Types of Ladybird Beetles (enlarged).
The small lines show their actual length.

Many insects, such as bees, assist in the pollination of flowers, and in that way help plants in the production of fruits and seeds.

Insects have many natural enemies, the chief of which are other insects, birds, reptiles, and fungi, and it will be well for us to make ourselves acquainted with them in order that we may know which to preserve and which to destroy. In some countries, where new insects have been introduced and have multiplied so rapidly as to become plant pests, it has been found possible to control them by bringing their natural enemies also from the native country of the pest.

Plant lice, or aphides, are destroyed in large numbers by ladybird beetles. The larvæ of the lacewing and hover-flies also feed upon them. In the picture you will see a lacewing larva capturing a thrips larva. Thrips, as you know, are a common insect pest.

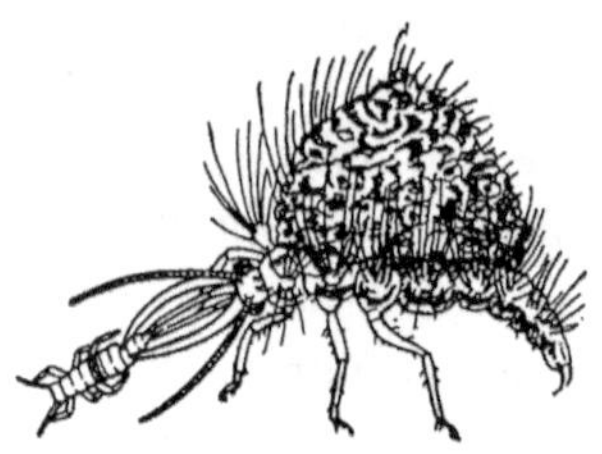

Larva of Lacewing Fly capturing a Thrips Larva (enlarged).

The Jack Spaniard and other wasps,* although certainly not friendly to man, are of considerable value in the garden, as they feed on caterpillars of all kinds, which are often greedy pests. In St. Vincent and other cotton-growing islands they are of much value in controlling the cotton-worm.

Jack Spaniard.

Both the dragon-fly and the praying mantis are insect eaters. Dragon-flies are often brightly coloured, with large transparent wings. They may be seen darting about in the air or over water, catching flies, mosquitoes, and butterflies very quickly, tearing them to pieces and devouring them

* In Belize all wasps are known as *wass-wass*.

without resting in their flight. The praying mantis is a frequent visitor to our houses at night, and it is interesting to see how cautiously it makes its way towards the insect it desires for its food; when close enough it makes a swift dart at it and eats it very quickly. We shall read more of this wonderful creature in Book V.

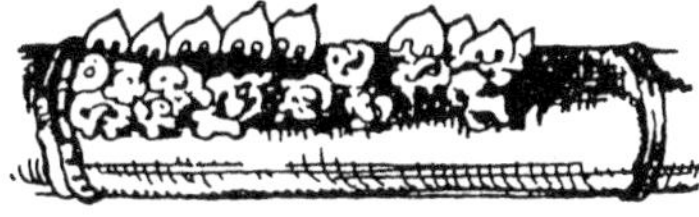

Scale Insects attached to the stem of a plant.

Several plant pests are controlled by insects which deposit their eggs in the eggs or in the larvæ or the caterpillars of the pest. These hatch out and destroy the eggs or larvæ in which they are laid by feeding on them. Well-known examples are the moth-borer of the sugarcane and the cotton-worm.

In Trinidad in recent years the insect known as the froghopper has done considerable damage to the sugarcane. These insects are checked to some extent by a green fungus which attacks the adults.

Many plants are attacked by scale insects, and these are also kept down in numbers in the same way by various kinds of fungi known by such names as the red-headed fungus and the white-headed fungus. Examine some scale insects on lime or guava trees and you will no doubt discover these fungi. If you were to spray the scale insects with a poisonous liquid to destroy them you would probably kill the fungus as well. In such cases it is best to find out to what extent the pest is

Scale Insect, young or crawling stage (enlarged).

being controlled by its natural enemies such as this before we adopt artificial means such as spraying with insecticides.

Corn-bird, or Yellow-tail.

Frogs and toads are well known to be friends of plants, as they live upon worms, slugs, caterpillars, and insects which do much damage to plants. In England cucumbers and many other plants which we grow out of doors have to be reared in glasshouses. A few frogs or toads are therefore placed in the glass-houses to assist in limiting the plant pests. Lizards are also garden friends, as they feed on insects.

Although we have left birds till last, they must not be considered the least useful of plant friends. It is true that some, such as the corn-bird or yellow-tail, can do much damage to our corn crop, and that many take a share of our fruit crop. It is also true, however, that they feed largely on insects and the seeds of weeds. In countries where the plough is largely used to till the ground, it is a familiar sight to see birds following quite close to it, searching for worms, grubs, insects, and weed seeds for food.

King of the Woods.

Most birds, however, are more useful than harmful. Hawks and owls occasionally take toll of our young chickens and other domestic birds, but they also feed on rats, mice, and insects, which in their turn might do a vast amount of damage in the cane-fields and on cacao estates.

Keskidee.

Many birds are insect-eaters, and it is an amusing sight on wet afternoons, when flying ants are prevalent, to see the birds darting from trees, collecting and devouring these insects. The cacao beetle, which is a serious pest of the cacao tree in the West Indies, is also destroyed by some birds. The principal one is that beautiful bird of which we read in Book II., the "king of the woods," or boo-too-too. Others which are useful in keeping down this pest are the black vulture *(merle corbeau)* and the keskidee (*qu'est-ce-qu'il-dit*). Woodpeckers also may be seen climbing the trees and picking out the caterpillars.

Woodpecker.

It is generally supposed that humming-birds visit flowers for the purpose of obtaining the nectar. They are, however, almost entirely insect-eaters, and they visit flowers for the purpose of finding small insects.

Finally, we must not forget that our domestic birds, such as fowls and ducks, feed upon insects to some extent. They are certainly bad gardeners, and do much damage if allowed to scratch or trample upon the garden beds when plants are growing in them, but they are useful in picking up mole-crickets, caterpillars, and other insects.

You will now understand that although plants are subject to very many pests and diseases, Nature has provided in turn various ways by which these pests can be checked or kept in control. If from thoughtlessness or ignorance we destroy those means which Nature has supplied, the pests will continue unchecked, and the plants may be destroyed on a large scale, whilst we shall suffer by reaping smaller crops.

Exercises

1. *Insecticides* are substances used *to kill insects.* Which part of the word means "to kill"?
   What, therefore, do the following words mean: infanticide, suicide, patricide, homicide?
2. Add as many names as you can to this list of plant friends, and then complete the other column.

Plant friends.	Ways in which they are of value.
Bees	Help to pollinate flowers .
Ladybird beetles .	. . . .
. . . .	. . . .
. . . .	. . . .
etc.	etc.

3. What do you mean by the "control of insects"? What other expressions (having a similar meaning) are used in this lesson?

4. Study these words: fungus (*singular*); fungi (*plural*). What other words do you know that change in this way?
5. Make a list of the twelve words you find most difficult to spell in this lesson. Learn them thoroughly.
6. Fill in the blanks:
   (*a*) Some insects are the —— of man, as they help him to —— his enemies.
   (*b*) The —— mantis often has the same —— as the plants on which it sits, and is therefore not—— to see.
   (c) The —— fly is one of the most —— insects we have. It generally lives near ——, over which it darts with lightning —— to —— its prey.
   (*d*) Aphides are curious little ——. They get their living easily, so, like a man who does not have to work for his ——, they do not —— very far.
   (*e*) —— are birds which live on the trunks of ——. You can often —— them tapping the bark with their hard —— to drive out the —— from the little crevices.
   (*f*) Birds are both —— and —— of man. In the first case they destroy his ——, but in the second they devour many harmful —— which —— his crops.

Humming-bird.

LESSON 37

THE BUCCANEERS—II

ALTHOUGH Drake and the others of his time were called buccaneers, as we read in Lesson 21, they were not the type of ruffians or pirates which developed in later years in the days of "Blackbeard," or Teach, of whom we may read in a book called *Tom Cringle's Log*, and of that notorious scoundrel and cut-throat who in the old ballad sings boastfully:

"Oh, my name is Captain Kidd,
  And God's laws I did forbid,
And right wickedly I did,
  As I sailed."

It is another matter when we come to the doings of such buccaneers as this Teach and Kidd, Roberts, Avery, and the rest of their evil crew. These daring rovers, who infested the seas around the West Indies in the seventeenth century, were of all nationalities, though chiefly English and French. They made Jamaica their headquarters and called themselves the "Brethren of the Coast," and were bound by the strongest oaths of loyalty to one another.

Their property was held in common, and "as they had no domestic ties—neither wife nor child, brother nor sister, being known among the buccaneers—the want of family relations was supplied by strict comradeship. Their chief virtue was courage." Their dress consisted of a "shirt dipped in the blood of the animals they killed; a pair of drawers dirtier than the shirt; a leathern girdle in which a small cutlass was hung and several knives; a hat without a rim, but with a small peak in front; and shoes without stockings."

The Governor of Jamaica was only too glad to receive these wild and lawless rovers of the sea; for he was in constant dread of the attacks of the Spaniards, of whom the buccaneers were sworn enemies. It was by their aid that two attempts made by the Spaniards from San Domingo to recover the island were frustrated. Their robbery of the Spanish treasure-ships brought abundance of money to the island, by which the settlers did not hesitate to profit. It is, therefore, to these bold buccaneers that Britain owes the possession and prosperity of her largest West Indian colony.

The natives of the islands which had not been colonized by Spain looked upon the pirates as their friends and avengers; the sympathy of the Caribs, indeed, was entirely with them, for a deadly hatred against Spain, had arisen because of the cold-blooded cruelty with which the first inhabitants of these islands had been treated. For this cruelty, therefore, the Spaniards were now made to pay a bitter penalty, for the buccaneers could always count on native support, and so did not hesitate to attack large towns by land when they had swept the sea clear of their Spanish foes.

It became a common custom for the Spaniards to seize their money and goods at the first sight of the pirate flag, and to flee to the woods for their lives. Thousands perished every year, and the destruction of life and property was a severe check to Spanish trade in these seas.

"FIERCELY AND LONG THIS GALLANT MAN FOUGHT."

(See page 205.)

One of the most notable of those buccaneers was a Welshman named Henry Morgan. Earlier in his life he was a white slave in Barbados, whither he had been kidnapped and shipped for work in the plantations, but managed to escape and join the pirate band. He was a most daring and desperate character, and succeeded in what seem to us almost impossible enterprises.

In one of these he determined to storm the flourishing town of Porto Bello, near the Isthmus of Panama. The city itself was easily taken by his crew of pirates, but the fort was a harder nut to crack. Here the Governor himself, a most gallant Spanish gentleman, was in command; inspired by his example the garrison fought bravely, and the buccaneers for a time made slight impression and lost heavily.

But Morgan was not to be denied. Ladders wide enough to carry three or four men abreast were hastily made; priests and nuns who had been made prisoners were compelled to plant these against the walls of the fort, Morgan supposing that the Governor would not order his men to fire on such bearers. But the Governor was of stern stuff, and had sworn that never would he be taken alive. The priests and nuns were not spared, though they cried piteously to him to surrender the fort and thus to save both his own and their lives. The ladders were planted, a wild rush was made, and the buccaneers swarmed up; and after a prolonged and bitter struggle the Spanish garrison threw down their arms and sued for quarter.

Not so the Governor. Fiercely and long this gallant man fought on regardless of hopeless odds, killing not only many of the buccaneers, but even slaying with his sword some of his own men who refused to fight longer. With his back to the rampart, his restless sword flickered here

SIR HENRY MORGAN.
(From an old engraving.)

and darted there, till in front of him rose a wall of dead and dying. In vain his wife and his daughter with tears besought him to yield; in vain the buccaneers offered him quarter; he but fought the more fiercely in answer to all appeals, and his sole reply in words was: "I had rather die as a valiant soldier than be hanged as a coward." To the credit of the buccaneers it is recorded that they endeavoured to take him alive, but he defended himself so obstinately that they were forced to kill him. So fell a most gallant gentleman. Had the Spaniards in the West Indies been led by such heroes, the task of Drake and his successors might not have been accomplished.

Thus the treasure of the richest and most populous town in America was carried off to Jamaica, and the city was afterwards burnt to the ground.

On another occasion Morgan sacked the town of Panama itself. As they neared the city, a large Spanish force, nearly three times their own strength, blocked the way of the buccaneers. Horse, foot, and artillery were there, and to make their work the more easy, the Spaniards had brought with them a vast herd of wild bulls to drive down on the ranks of their assailants, so as to break them up and ensure a simple task for the cavalry. But the buccaneers cared nothing for wild bulls, and the leading ones were shot, as, driven forward by mounted Indians, they came routing and thundering along; the rest, mad with panic, wheeled round and charged through the Spanish army, overthrowing horses, breaking up the ranks in utter confusion, trampling men to death—doing, in fact, to the Spaniards exactly what the Spaniards had planned they should do to their opponents.

On the heels of the maddened bulls came the cheering buccaneers. Two hours saw six hundred Spanish dead lying in the field, and the remainder in desperate flight;

by afternoon the pirates were in possession of the city, and they found in the wells and caves of the neighbouring district an almost incredible amount of hidden treasure which was carried off to Jamaica.

Meantime a treaty had been made between Britain and Spain, and the Governor of the island declined to allow it to be broken. So Morgan took to a more peaceful trade, became a planter, and later on was made a knight, and was three times governor of the island which had been the headquarters of his pirate raids.

Exercises

1. Explain the difference between the first "buccaneers," such as Hawkins and Drake, and those of the following century, such as Morgan and Kidd. Which were adventurers, and which were pirates or freebooters?
2. Where was the headquarters of the pirates? Why was the governor of that place glad to receive them?
3. Were the pirates friendly with the Caribs? If so, explain why; if not, give reasons.
4. Describe in your own words the attack on Porto Bello.
5. Give an illustration from this lesson of the old saying, "The biter bitten."
6. The word "buccaneer" is derived from the simple "boucan," used by hunters for drying their meat. Do you think this was a fitting name for these desperate characters?
7. Make sentences of your own containing the following words:

notorious	domestic	enterprises	confusion
nationalities	virtue	gallant	knight
loyalty	hesitate	endeavoured	besought

"ON THE HEELS OF THE MADDENED BULLS CAME THE CHEERING BUCCANEERS."

(*See page 207.*)

LESSON 38

A VISIT TO AN ARROWROOT ESTATE IN ST. VINCENT

I

SCHOOL had closed for the Christmas vacation, and Allan Smith was to spend his holidays on his uncle's estate in the island of St. Vincent. Of all his studies plant life interested him most, and he had longed for this opportunity to learn something about the arrowroot plant and its manufacture.

After a delightful motor drive along the beautiful windward coast of the island, he was warmly greeted by his uncle, who had not seen him for some time.

"How well you look, Allan, and how tall you have grown," said his uncle, as he grasped his hand. "You have come at a favourable time, as the arrowroot crop is ready, and we are reaping and manufacturing to-day."

"Oh, how fortunate, uncle," replied Allan; "I have been wanting to learn all about that interesting plant."

"Well," said his uncle, "let us first visit the field where the reaping is being done."

A busy scene presented itself, for there were the labourers, men and women, working merrily, while they chatted and poked fun at each other. The men were digging with their hoes, while the women walked behind them, taking up the starch-laden "roots," as they are called, and collecting them into little heaps ready to be carried to the works.

Rhizomes of Arrowroot gathered into heaps.

"Why does that man occasionally throw back a piece of the plant into the soil and cover it over?" asked Allan.

"He is planting the crop for next season," was the answer.—"Here, John," his uncle called to one of the men, "dig up a plant, and hand it to me."

He then began to explain the nature of the plant.

"This plant," he said, "is similar in growth to the grass family, of which I know you have read in the First Book of your West Indian Readers. It grows from a rhizome. Do you see this upright green stem which appears above the ground?" asked Mr. Smith.

"Yes," answered Allan, "and I notice also that there are horizontal colourless stalks with buds, nodes, and internodes similar to those one sees in the sugarcane plant. I know from my Nature-study lessons that these stalks must grow underground, or the light of the sun would turn them green. I observe, too, that the upright green stalks grow out from these, forming a shape like the letter L."

Arrowroot Plant and "Roots."

"Exactly" said his uncle; "that is what a rhizome means. At the base of each upright stem a bud develops underground, and grows parallel to the surface of the ground for a certain distance. Its tip then curls upwards to form another upright stem, and the process is repeated again and again. The roots, found in a bunch at the base of the upright stem, and the leaves supply the food material, which is passed into the underground stems and stored up, principally in the form of starch. When the plant is dug up, the lower portion of the upright stem, with a part of the horizontal stem, is thrown back into the soil as a cutting."

"I see now what the man was doing," said Allan, his face gleaming with interest. "How is it that the leaves have lost their green colour, and hang down as if they are about to drop off?"

"They have done their work," explained Mr. Smith, "and the underground stems—or 'roots,' as they are sometimes wrongly termed—are now fully packed with starch. That is how we know when the time for reaping has come. This occurs about eleven months after the crop has been planted."

Young Plant growing from Rhizome.

"Where are those women carrying the baskets?"

"They are taking the 'roots' to the works to be ground and to have the starch extracted. From more distant fields they are brought in by carts. Let us walk to the works and see what is being done there."

"What a quantity of water there is around here!" said Allan in surprise.

"Yes," said his uncle, "water is one of the chief needs in the manufacture, and it must be pure and cool. Hence it is filtered, if possible, through sand-beds."

They watched the women throw the "roots" into a bath to be first washed and then passed through a revolving wooden cylinder where the water gave them a second washing. Allan followed these processes with interest, and was then attracted by a man standing near to a rapidly-revolving wheel.

"What is he doing?" he asked.

Washing the Rhizomes.

"He is working the *grater,*" said his uncle. "Note how he takes the 'roots' and presses them against the rim of the wheel with part of a coconut leaf stem, rapidly reducing them to pulp. Notice also how like a grater the surface of the wheel looks.

"Look over there," continued Mr. Smith. "That set of sieves of fine mesh, arranged in tiers or rows above each other, are the strainers, in which the pulp is washed and squeezed over and over again till all the starch is extracted."

"Why are the pipes covered with bags at the nozzles?"

"The water is being filtered once more so as to render it as pure as possible before it is used to wash the pulp."

"What is done with the starch when it leaves the sieves? I notice that it is carried away in a trough."

"We will go to another part of the works and see what happens," said his uncle.

Just then the estate bell rang for the breakfast hour, and Mr. Smith and Allan went into the house to enjoy a good meal after their busy morning.

Washing the Starch: Settling Trough in the foreground.

II

While Allan was sitting on the verandah after breakfast, chatting with his uncle and aunt, the bell once more rang for work to be resumed, and Mr. Smith led his nephew away to another part of the works to show him what was done with the starch after it had been passed through the sieves.

There a very different scene met their eyes.

"This looks like a large bath," said Allan, pointing to a receptacle about fifty feet long and twenty wide.

"Yes," agreed his uncle, "and into this bath the washed starch is led from the sieves by the trough whose end you see above."

Allan noticed that a wall ran along the centre of the bath from one end to within two feet of the other, while barriers were placed at intervals, dividing the bath into sections. Noting his look of inquiry, Mr. Smith promptly supplied the needed information.

"This bath is called a *settler*, for here the starch becomes separated from the water and sinks to the bottom. There is a slight current which flows out at one end of the settler. The starch slowly sinks to the bottom, but portions get carried on until they meet the barriers, which are really sieves. The liquid is there further strained to remove impurities. After this settling process has continued for some time the starch is removed, and placed into the concrete tubs you see along the side of the room. There it is again washed and stirred to remove further impurities. Any sand which may be present in the starch sinks to the bottom of the tub and is dug out when the starch has settled. This settling takes place overnight, and the starch is removed next morning."

"What is that thick, dark scum which the man is removing with a kind of wooden ladle and putting aside?"

"That comes from the gummy matter of the rind of the 'roots,' and on settling it produces an impure form of starch known as *madongo.*"

"What now becomes of the washed starch?"

"It is dug out of the tubs, after the removal of any impurities. The starch then forms a hard block, which is broken into lumps and taken to another part of the building to be dried. Let us go and see how this is done."

They ascended to an upper floor, and there, in a draughty room, the drying process was being carried out.

"What is that framework with layers of wide-meshed wire placed one above the other?" asked Allan.

Drying House: Lumps of Starch on wire netting.

"Those are the driers," said his uncle. "The lumps of starch are placed on the wire mesh, and as they dry they crumble and fall into the large wooden tray you see underneath. The small dried lumps are now ready to be packed into barrels. Here we see a man doing the packing."

"Why is he using that heavy stick, and placing blue tissue-paper as a lining inside the barrel?" Allan inquired.

"The stick is used as a rammer, so that the barrel may be tightly packed, while the blue paper protects the arrowroot from impure gases, which would be readily absorbed by the starch. The barrel is finally covered down and ready for shipment."

"All that has been very interesting, uncle; but what are the uses of arrowroot" asked Allan.

Packing Arrowroot.

"Many and various," was the prompt reply. "The fibrous matter—locally known as *bitty*—left over from the squeezed pulp is used like the *megasse* of the sugar-cane to make paper, or for making mattresses. The *madongo* is cooked by the labourers as a substitute for flour dumplings. The greater part of the arrowroot is shipped for sale abroad, where it is largely used in the making of biscuits, cakes, and confectionery, and in the preparation of many patent foods. The pure starch is used locally as food for infants and invalids, and for making cakes, puddings, sauces, blancmange, and other things. In case of a sore, an arrowroot poultice is particularly useful, as it draws, cleanses, and heals the wound."

While this explanation was being given they had been walking homewards and now entered the house, Allan thinking over all the interesting things he had heard in connection with the marvellous arrowroot plant.

St. Vincent enjoys a world-wide reputation for arrowroot, and is one of the few places where the plant can be cultivated successfully on a large scale. The island has a light loamy soil, well-drained and easily worked, while the large quantities of pure water necessary in the manufacture are available in the mountain streams.

The merits of the product were well advertised, and the great care taken in the manufacture and packing of the starch demonstrated, at the St. Vincent section of the West Indian Pavilion at Wembley, England, and in similar exhibitions elsewhere. Pamphlets describing the uses of this important food were freely distributed. Samples packed in miniature barrels were also presented to visitors. As a result, several important grocery firms in England have begun to import and retail this useful commodity.

Exercises

1. How many questions did Allan ask? Are there any points in the growth of the plant or its manufacture that you do not understand? If so, what other questions would you like to ask?
2. There are several words in this lesson which sometimes cause difficulty in their spelling. Learn them carefully. They are:
   parallel, piece, similar, principally, sieves, verandah, scene, trough, centre, separated, stirred, ascended, draughty, poultice, preparation, marvellous, pamphlets, and miniature.
3. What island is especially famous for its arrowroot? What advantages has this island in the cultivation of this plant? To what group of the British West Indies does this island belong? What is its chief town?

4. What are the following?—
   strainers, graters, settlers, madongo, bitty, megasse, rhizome.
5. Fill in the blanks:
   (*a*) The estate was in the —— part of the island.
   (*b*) The plant relies on its —— and —— for its food supply.
   (*c*) The roots are washed —— times. Altogether they pass through —— processes in the works.
   (*d*) The plant is similar to the —— —— in ——.
   (*e*) The object of all the operations is to obtain the —— from the —— stems in as —— a form as possible.
   (*f*) The barrel is —— with blue —— ——.
   (*g*) The plant is said to be so named because the Indians of South America used it to cure their —— caused by poisoned ——.

LESSON 39

PICTURE LESSONS—X

The Sheepfold

In the picture on page 221 we have an effect of moonlight which we may have often seen, but which most of us would, find it impossible to show on paper or canvas.

If we examine the picture carefully we shall see that there is not very much drawing in it. Even the flock of sheep, which is the most important part of the picture, does not seem to have any very definite shape.

Yet no one, not even the youngest of us, requires to be told the title of the picture. Because the picture shows no special definite form or any decided colour, would it therefore be easy to paint?

THE SHEEPFOLD.
(*Jean-François Millet, 1814–75.*)

It is only when we begin to look at it very carefully that we see how the artist has created something very true and very real out of almost nothing. As we look more closely, things begin to take shape just as they do at night. Hold the picture some distance away from you and it will seem very real.

If we look at the sky first, we will notice that the moon is not sharply and clearly defined, nor is it white. Next we notice that it is not round—in other words, it is not full moon.

We also see it has a halo round it, but it is so delicate and so faint that we can just see it and no more.

Notice the patches of cloud in the sky; some are silver-edged, and some without any light striking on them.

The hut, the sheep-pen, the man, the sheep, and the dog are all ghostly. We can see the moonlight streaming over the backs of the sheep, but we cannot see very clearly where their legs end or if they have any feet.

What we know about sheep, or anything else, is not what the artist sees, and if we were looking at this scene in real life we would be sure to pass by and not notice much that the artist has painted in his picture.

We do, however, see the shepherd more or less clearly, with outstretched arm directing the sheep through the gate into the fold. Or is he striking something—perhaps fixing the fence?

Only an artist like Millet could have painted such a picture and got such an effect as this. We can think of him, standing in the fields studying the scene. Then, as soon as he is indoors, he takes out his sketchbook and makes notes of what he has seen. Some of these notes are written and some drawn.

During the next day he thinks a good deal about the picture he intends to paint. He may visit the scene in daytime, but how different it looks! No silver moon, no ghostly forms, no mystery.

Then in the evening he comes back and studies it all over again. When he has got it thoroughly into his mind he probably paints it from memory.

In this picture, therefore, we see not only the scene as the artist saw it, but also as he thought about it. The artist has shown us in this picture several things he found out by studying the scene.

One of them is that the natural colours of grass, sheep's wool, and almost everything else, disappear in moonlight.

A second thing he has shown us is that in a dull or weak light we do not see the edges of things clearly— they appear soft and dimly defined.

Those are two things which the artist remembered when he was painting his picture. When next we have an opportunity we should see whether he was right about these two points.

LESSON 40

COMMON HARMFUL PLANTS

SOME plants are decidedly harmful, not only to other forms of plant life, but also to human beings. Long before we begin to make a special study of plant life we learn almost unconsciously which fruits and other parts of plants are good for food and which are poisonous or unfit to eat.

Poisonous plants are generally regarded as harmful, but we must remember that man can make use of some of these poisons in various ways, such as in medicine and for insecticides for spraying plant pests.

In the West Indies we have several plants which are well known to you as poisonous. The "cactus-hedge" which surrounds many gardens and fields has an abundance of milky sap which will cause blindness if it gets into the eyes. The manchineel, a common tree on many of our seashores, is always avoided because of the painful blisters which the milky sap will cause on the skin. The akee, a common Jamaican fruit which is much liked by the people of that island, is delicious when picked in a ripe condition and properly prepared; dropped or over-ripe fruits, however, have caused serious cases of poisoning and occasionally death has been the result.

"Cactus-Hedge."

There are some plants also which are poisonous to stock. The oleander, one of our pretty garden shrubs, is fatal to animals such as cows and horses, if they feed upon it. Some wild plants, such as Brinvillers, are also commonly said to be poisonous to stock.

There are many plants which you know by the name of "cow-itch" whose irritating hairs give us considerable trouble to get rid of if we handle them. There are also the stinging nettles, which cause considerable pain if they come into contact with the bare skin.

Matapalo encircling and smothering a tree.

In addition to these types of harmful plants there are some trees and plants which grow upon others and sometimes entirely smother them. The name matapalo or Scotch Attorney is no doubt familiar to you. These trees, of which there are several kinds, often commence their existence as seedlings in the forks of other trees, sending later their long aerial roots down to the ground. Eventually they will entirely encircle and kill the supporting tree, although they do not actually take food from it.

In the picture of this plant you will see how the long straight roots have gone down to the ground and how other roots are tightly clasping the trunk of the host tree. It is necessary to examine frequently trees which we value, to see that the matapalos do not destroy them in this way. Trees of this kind will also grow in old masonry, causing much damage, and they are difficult to destroy if not taken out when quite young.

Oleander.

The bird-vine, vage, or mistletoe is one of the most troublesome pests to the cacao planter. It can also do much damage on many kinds of trees beside the cacao, such as the orange, the mango, and the lime. This plant does not send roots into the ground, but obtains its water and mineral substances entirely from the host tree on which it is growing. It is really a *semi*-parasite, as it only takes water and mineral salts from its host; it makes the remaining part of its food by means of its own green leaves.

This harmful vine produces attractive little berries, and these are eaten by birds, which spread them to other trees, either by cleaning their beaks upon the trees, or by eating the berries and passing the seeds through their bodies. The seeds germinate and push their little roots right into the branch of the tree on which they are growing. The plants then make a complete union with the host tree and live upon the food collected by the roots of their host.

Bird-Vine, or Mistletoe.

The bird-vine or mistletoe is often of a rambling or bushy habit. The plants grow rapidly, and soon smother and weaken the host tree if they are not cut out. If they are allowed to develop, the branches of the tree on which they are growing have also to be cut off if the pest is to be eradicated. So troublesome are the various kinds of mistletoe to the planter that he often has to employ a gang of men to destroy them. In some islands the Government makes it compulsory for people who own land to keep their trees clear of this pest.

Love-Vine, or Dodder.

Another kind of plant which smothers is the love-vine or dodder. It is a common pest of hibiscus hedges, and has orange-coloured, thread-like stems without leaves, with small inconspicuous flowers. Unlike the bird-vine, this plant begins its life on the ground where the seeds germinate. Its roots die as soon as the tiny plant has become attached to the hibiscus or other host plant. After this it becomes a *total* parasite, living upon the sap of the plant to which it is attached.

Water Hyacinth: Flower.

Besides growing from seed it will also grow readily from small pieces of the stem, so you must be careful not to play with pieces and throw them on to other plants. Love-vine is more conspicuous than bird-vine, but it is not nearly so harmful as a pest. It is destroyed by cutting out and burning those parts of the host plant on which it is growing, or sometimes by spraying with certain poisonous liquids.

The pretty water hyacinth, which floats on fresh water with its roots attached to the mud, is a serious pest in the southern states of America, India, Ceylon, Australia, and other countries. It chokes up canals and other slow-moving waterways.

There are other plants which, although not directly harmful themselves, form a suitable harbour for other forms of life which are harmful. In this group are the wild pines and balisier, which hold water, either in the leaves or in parts of the flower. Mosquitoes lay their eggs in this water, and the larvæ grow and later develop into fully-grown insects.

In Lesson 22 we saw that many plants are harmful as weeds, some actually being a menace to cultivation and pastures in various countries.

Exercises

1. Make a list of the various ways in which plants may be harmful. Give examples in each case.
2. Explain the difference between a *semi*-parasite and a *total* parasite. Illustrate your answer by reference to the bird-vine and the love-vine.
3. How are these plants spread?—Scotch Attorney, bird-vine, and love-vine.
4. A "host" is a person who entertains a stranger, or guest, at his house without reward. In what ways do the trees and plants described in the lesson as "hosts" resemble him?
5. "Out of evil may come much good." Give an illustration of this from the lesson.
6. Fill in the blanks:
   (*a*) The root-cap which a plant has at the tip of its —— is often not easy to ——. It can easily be seen, however, on —— of the water ——, that pretty plant which is a serious —— in some ——.
   (*b*) The —— of the ——, which grows by the seashore, causes —— if it is dropped on the skin.
   (*c*) The —— or —— is a parasite which has no ——. It is often found injuring lime and other ——.
   (*d*) Parasitic plants give off a liquid which dissolves a way for them into the —— plant.
   (e) The —— vine obtains all its food from the host, but the —— vine makes part of its own by means of its ——.

LESSON 41

THE DIAMOND OF THE DESERT

Note.—The time of this story was A.D. 1190, about three hundred years before Columbus discovered the New World.

FAR away in the land of Palestine, which we also call the Holy Land, a Scottish Knight, who had joined the army of Crusaders under the gallant King of England, Richard Lion Heart, was riding slowly by the shores of the Dead Sea in the burning midday sun.

All the morning, through rocky and dangerous narrow passes, he had come, till he had reached the great plain where the Dead Sea lies—so desolate a place that never a bird is seen to fly for miles around, nor does any green thing ever grow.

The Knight was clothed in armour from head to foot, and wore a steel breastplate and a pair of iron gloves. From his belt, on one side, hung a long broad double-edged sword, with a handle in the form of a cross; and on the other side a stout dagger.

Over his armour, to keep away the burning rays of the sun, he also wore an overcoat of embroidered cloth, which was frayed at the edges and much worn, and on which the Knight's arms were borne in several places—a sleeping leopard, with the motto, "I sleep —wake me not."

He also carried a long steel-headed lance, from the top of which flew a little flag, and the lance was secured to his saddle, with one end resting on his stirrup.

His horse, too, was clothed in heavy armour, with a steel axe hanging from the saddle-bow.

The Crusader was glad to leave this desolate place, and when he had left it some distance behind, he saw, with joy, a little cluster of palm trees, and guessed that they grew by a well, where he had been directed to take his midday rest.

His good horse, too, tired and thirsty like his master, snuffed up the air as if he smelt the water, and began to quicken his pace over the loose, heavy sand.

But as the Knight of the Leopard looked longingly at the palm trees that were still a little distance off, he thought he saw some object moving among the trees, and, as he strained his eyes, he soon saw that it was a mounted horseman.

The mounted horseman must have seen him too, for he came riding towards the Knight at a tremendous speed. And the Crusader knew, from the turban which the stranger wore, the long spear, and the green caftan—a long-sleeved, loose vest tied about the waist with a girdle—that the horseman was a Saracen cavalier. "Saracen" was the name given by the Crusaders to Easterns and Muslims.

Faster and faster rode the Saracen on a beautiful Barbary horse; and the Knight of the Leopard, taking his lance from the saddle, and seizing it in his right hand, put spurs to his steed, ready to encounter the stranger.

The Saracen earned on his left arm a light, round shield, made of the skin of the rhinoceros, ornamented with silver loops, and grasped his long spear with his right hand, and brandished it above his head.

The Knight of the Leopard, knowing how tired his good horse was, instead of riding to meet the stranger, now made a dead halt, feeling that his own weight and that of his powerful charger could best meet this enemy standing.

The Saracen evidently thought so too, for when he had approached the Knight to within the distance of six or seven yards, he cleverly wheeled his horse to the left, and rode twice round his adversary. But the Knight kept turning his horse as well, so that his face was turned constantly towards his foe, who had no opportunity to attack him on an unguarded point.

The Saracen next retreated to the distance of about a hundred yards, and then, like a hawk attacking a heron, he again rode round and round the Knight, but with no better success.

A third time the Saracen approached in the same manner, when the Knight of the Leopard, wishing to end this uncertain sort of warfare, suddenly seized the steel axe hanging at his saddle-bow, and, with a strong hand and splendid aim, hurled it against the Saracen's head.

Swiftly the Saracen raised his light shield, and though it kept the axe from striking his head, the violence of the blow forced the shield down on his turban, and the Mahometan was thrown from his horse. But so quick was he that before the Knight could reach him, the foe had sprung nimbly to his feet, and calling his steed, which instantly ran to his side, the Arab leaped into his seat without touching the stirrup.

In the meantime the Knight had recovered his axe; but the Saracen, remembering the skill and strength with which his adversary had aimed it, took good care to keep out of its reach.

"A THIRD TIME THE SARACEN APPROACHED IN THE SAME MANNER."

(*See page 232.*)

Retiring to some little distance, the Saracen now planted his long spear in the sand, and taking a bow which he carried at his back, he strung it, and putting his horse to the gallop, he again circled round the Knight, but at a greater distance off; and as he galloped, he discharged six arrows one after the other at the Knight, and with such excellent aim, that every arrow struck his foe, and the Crusader would have been wounded six times over had it not been for the strength of his armour.

Again the Arab shot a seventh arrow, and this last must have entered a less perfect part of the armour, for the Knight dropped heavily from his horse. The Saracen dismounted at once, and went to examine his fallen adversary. But his surprise was great when he found himself in an iron grasp; for the Crusader, who had only pretended that he was wounded, flung out his hand, and clutched him by the sword-belt.

The wily Saracen immediately unbuckled the belt, and, springing away again, mounted his horse, which seemed to watch his master's movements with the intelligence of a human being. But the Saracen had now lost his sword and his quiver of arrows as well, for they were attached to the sword-belt; and thinking, perhaps, that it would be better to have this valiant Christian as a friend than as a foe, the Mahometan approached the Crusader with his right hand held out quite in a friendly fashion.

"There is a truce between our nations," he said in the mixed language which the Arabs and the Europeans used when they spoke together; "wherefore should there be war betwixt thee and me? Let there be peace between us."

For at this time the leaders of the Crusade, who were encamped with their followers near the town of Acre, on the coast of Palestine, had just made a truce with Saladin, the great Sultan of Egypt and Syria. It was he against whom they had been fighting for the possession of the Holy Sepulchre, which, as you know, is the grave where the Body of our Saviour had been laid.

"I am well contented," answered the Knight of the Leopard; "but what security dost thou offer that thou wilt keep the truce?"

"The word of a follower of the Prophet Mahomet was never broken," answered the Saracen proudly. "It is thou, brave Christian, from whom I should ask security, did I not know that treason seldom dwells with courage."

"By the cross of my sword," said the Crusader, laying his hand on the weapon as he spoke, "I will be true companion to thee, Saracen."

"By Mahomet, Prophet of God, and by Allah, God of the Prophet, there is not treachery in my heart towards thee," replied the Saracen. "And now let us go to yonder fountain, for the hour of rest is at hand."

And the two warriors, who had tried so lately to kill each other, rode side by side, without an angry look or sign of doubt, to the little cluster of palm trees.

It was a beautiful spot; the grass under the palms was like a carpet of green velvet, and looked still more beautiful by contrast with the barren desert around. The fountain had been walled in and arched over to keep the clouds of dust from settling upon the water, and to keep the burning sun from the cool, refreshing spring.

Here the tired warriors took saddle, bit, and rein from their noble steeds, and first let them drink from a marble basin into which the water always trickled, and then turned them loose, after which they themselves drank from the fountain under the arch.

Then they sat down together on the grass, and producing the small allowance each carried with him for his own refreshment, the men began their scanty meal. Each was naturally curious about the other, and each eyed the other with interest.

"Brave Nazarene," the Saracen cried—Nazarene was the name the Easterns gave to the Christians—"it were better for thyself to turn thy horse's head towards the camp of thy people, for to travel towards Jerusalem without a passport is but a wilful casting away of thy life."

"I have a pass," answered the Knight; and he produced a parchment, adding, "under Saladin's hand and seal."

The Saracen bent his head to the dust as he recognized the seal of the Sultan. He kissed the paper with great respect, pressed it to his forehead, and then returned it to the Knight.

"Rash man," he said, "thou hast sinned against thine own blood and mine for not showing this to me when we met."

"You came with levelled spear," said the Knight. "Had a troop of Saracens so attacked me, it might have stood with my honour to show the Sultan's pass, but never to *one* man."

"And yet one man," said the Saracen haughtily, "was enough to interrupt your journey."

"True, brave Mahometan," replied the Christian "but there are few such as thou art."

The Saracen looked pleased at the compliment. "But," said he, "well was it for me that I failed to slay thee, with the safeguard of the mighty Saladin upon thy person. My guilt had justly been avenged with cord or sabre."

"I am glad to hear that its power shall thus avail me," said the Knight, "for I have heard that the road is full of robber tribes who care for nothing if they can get plunder."

"The truth has been told to thee, brave Christian," said the Saracen.

The warriors now arose from their place of brief rest, and courteously helped each other while they carefully replaced the harness from which they had relieved their trusty steeds, the horses, meanwhile, neighing and snuffing fondly round their masters.

Before the Crusader mounted he again moistened his lips, and dipped his hands in the fountain, saying, "I would I knew the name of this delicious fountain, that I might hold it in my grateful remembrance."

"In the Arabic language," answered the Saracen, "it is called by a name which means 'The Diamond of the Desert.'"

"And well is it so named," replied the Knight.

And then the warriors, mounting their horses, continued their journey across the sandy waste.

[This story has been retold for you from the opening chapters of one of Sir Walter Scott's well-known novels, *The Talisman*. If you would like to follow further the fortunes of the Knight and the Saracen, you can do so in the little book from which the lesson was taken. Perhaps, when you are older, you will then want to read the whole novel.]

Exercises

1. Study the picture on page 233. Which horseman is the Knight of the Leopard, and which the Saracen? How do you know?
2. You have now read about many things which happened in the years long ago. Place the following names in the order in which the people lived:

Nelson	Henry Morgan	Drake
Columbus	Raleigh	King Richard I.
Odysseus	Napoleon	Queen Elizabeth
The Knight of the Leopard	King Arthur of the Round Table	Private Woodcock of the R.W. Kent Regt.

   If any of them lived at the same time, bracket them together.
3. Why do you think the "Dead Sea" got that name?
4. How many people are mentioned in this lesson? Which character do you admire most? Why?
5. Make sentences of your own containing the following phrases:

from head to foot	his surprise was great
a little distance off	the intelligence of a human being
wheeled his horse	in a friendly fashion
in the same manner	like a carpet of green velvet
with such excellent aim	across the sandy waste.

6. How many Proper Nouns are there in this lesson? Make a list of them.
7. Describe how a similar combat might have been fought with present-day weapons.

READING TESTS AND EXERCISES

Note.—Teachers are reminded that they should compile additional tests of a similar nature to the following. This work gives excellent practice in revision and individual reading.

TEST I

Make an index as you did in Books II. and III., showing the names of Guyana, Belize and all the West Indies named in this book.

Which one is mentioned most frequently?

TEST II

What names of people occur in this book? Make an index of them.

TEST III

Write out the words in this book which tell you these things, giving the number of the page on which they are found:

(*a*) This was found out some time ago.
(*b*) The flowers can hardly be detected.
(*c*) A certain European nation has produced many travellers and explorers.
(*d*) It was made so for this special purpose.
(*e*) We saw a hive of industry before us.
(*f*) The strongest will last the longest.
(*g*) Methods invented by man.
(*h*) He ran with tremendous speed.

TEST IV

(*a*) Which prose selection in this book pleases you most? Say why.

(*b*) Which poetical selection (including those in the "Additional Poetry") do you prefer? Give reasons for your choice.

(*c*) Which is your favourite coloured picture in this book? Say why.

IN MEMORIAM.
(Sir J. Noel Paton, 1821–1901. By kind permission of Alexander Whitelaw, Esq., Kirkintilloch, Scotland.)

TEST V

Who spoke the following words?—

(1) "God's laws I did forbid."
(2) "Here was a great and goodly tree."
(3) "The reward! Land! I see land!"
(4) "There is a truce betwixt our nations."
(5) "A mighty pleasant way with him, has my mate Bill."
(6) "Give me, my men, but three days."
(7) "I presume you do not care for a second trial."
(8) "Thank God we are in Holland."

TEST VI

Name the author of each of the following quotations. Where do they occur?

(*a*) "Much converse do I find in thee."
(*b*) "A necklace strung out on the breast
Of the sea breathing low in a dream."
(*c*) "Thy cities shall with commerce shine."
(*d*) "This is the watching hour."
(*e*) "To pour for the city hunger
The milk from the country's breast."
(*f*) "I lose myself in the infinite main."
(*g*) "His plans soared up again like fire."

TEST VII

A Picture Test

The picture on page 240 shows an incident in what is known in history as the Indian Mutiny. Study the picture, and then answer the following questions:

What emotions do the faces of the people show? (Select from joy, fear, happiness, terror, distress, love, hatred, anxiety, pleasure, anger, sympathy, and reverence.)

How many groups of people are in the picture? Describe the groups. Why are those at the back smaller and fainter? What kind of soldiers are they?

What story has the artist to tell? Has he done it well?

Why is the little child not afraid?

Describe the expression on the face of the native nurse.

What is the principal colour which the artist has used in his picture? How many other colours do you see in it?

Would you call this picture the work of a realistic or an idealistic painter? Why?

Can you suggest an alternative title to sum up all that the artist has tried to convey?

TEST VIII*

Instructions.—In each question a fourth word is wanted which goes with the third word (in capitals) in the same way as the second word (in capitals) goes with the first. Look in the second line of each question for the word that is wanted; and draw a line under it. Do not write anything.

Examples

GOOD is to BAD as WHITE is to
CLEAN, BLACK, WICKED, RED.

BAKER is to BREAD as TAILOR is to
TAILORESS, CAKE, MAN, CLOTHES.

1. FATHER is to MOTHER as HUSBAND is to
RED, WIFE, GREEN, BUSINESS.
2. UP is to DOWN as HIGH is to
LOW, BOOK, COAL, DIFFICULTY.
3. PRINCE is to PRINCESS as KING is to
DUCHESS, CROWN, QUEEN, ROYAL.
4. PARENT is to CHILD as MOTHER is to
WIFE, MAID, DAUGHTER, SERVANT.
5. FIRE is to HOT as ICE is to
CREAM, WATER, SOLID, COLD.
6. EAT is to BREAD as DRINK is to
DRUNKARD, THROAT, CUP, WATER.
7. SITTING is to CHAIR as SLEEPING is to
WALKING, TIRED, BED, DREAM.

* This test is from collections of group-tests prepared for the National Institute of Industrial Psychology, and is taken from *Psychological Tests of Educable Capacity* (English Board of Education).

8. JANUARY is to DECEMBER as SUNDAY is to
TUESDAY, MONDAY, SATURDAY, WINTER.
9. FLYING is to BIRD as CREEPING is to
AEROPLANE, SNAIL, GROUND, FLOWER.
10. TEARS are to SORROW as LAUGHTER is to
JOY, SMILING, CRYING, MISERY.
11. SIGHT is to PICTURE as HEARING is to
SONG, COLOUR, EAR, SEEING.
12. EGG is to BIRD as SEED is to
PLOUGHMAN, FOWL, PLANT, WHEAT.
13. REMEMBER is to PAST as ANTICIPATE is to
FANCY, FUTURE, FORGET, PRESENT.
14. BEAR is to CUB as DOG is to
CAT, SPANIEL, PUPPY, KITTEN.
15. FACT is to FICTION as HISTORIAN is to
HISTORY, BOOK, NOVELIST, MATHEMATICIAN
16. BEAUTY is to ART as TRUTH is to
SCIENCE, MUSIC, ARTIST, LIAR.
17. ASLEEP is to AWAKE as DEAD is to
HEAD, CORPSE, ALIVE, MORTALITY.
18. FOOD is to MAN as FUEL is to
WOMAN, STEAM, ENGINE, VAPOUR.
19. SKY is to GROUND as CEILING is to
GAS, WALL, FLOOR, CHANDELIER.
20. SWEET is to HONEY as SOUR is to
SUGAR, SALT, VINEGAR, PEPPER.
21. HORSE is to MULE as DOCILE is to
RIDER, STUBBORN, DONKEY, MAN.
22. WHEN is to WHERE as TIME is to
HOW, WHY, SPACE, LENGTH.
23. MOTIVE is to METHOD as WHY is to
WHERE, MANNER, REASON, HOW.
24. CAUSE is to EFFECT as DISEASE is to
REASON, CONSEQUENCE, DEATH, LIFE.
25. THE DAY BEFORE YESTERDAY is to THE DAY AFTER TO-MORROW as SATURDAY is to
SUNDAY, MONDAY, WEDNESDAY, FRIDAY.

QUOTATIONS WORTH REMEMBERING

PERFECTION

Trifles make perfection, and perfection is no trifle.

MICHAEL ANGELO (1475–1564)

TRUTH

Speaking truth is like writing fair, it only comes by practice.

JOHN RUSKIN (1819–1900).

GOOD HUMOUR

A laugh is worth a hundred groans in any state of the market.

CHARLES LAMB (1755–1834).

KINDNESS

As the sun lightens the world, so let our loving-kindness make bright this house of our habitation.

R. L. STEVENSON (1850–94).

BOOKS

I

Books are lighthouses erected in the great sea of time.

E. P. WHIPPLE (1819–86).

II

Bread of flour is good; but there is bread, sweet as honey if we would eat it, in a good book.

JOHN RUSKIN (1819–1900).

A THOUGHT

The heights by great men reached and kept,
Were not attained by sudden flight;
But they, while their companions slept,
Were toiling upward in the night.

H. W. LONGFELLOW (1807–82).

SUNSET

When the pilgrim Sun is travelling o'er
The last blue hill, to gild a distant shore,
He leaves a freshness in the evening scene
That tells Creation where his steps have been.

E. B. BROWNING (1806–61).

THOUGHTLESS WORDS

Oh, many a shaft, at random sent,
Finds mark the archer little meant,
And many a word at random spoken
May soothe, or wound, a heart that's broken!

SIR WALTER SCOTT (1771–1832).

DUTY

I tell you—it may be for the hundredth time, but it is the very truth—that this is the working day; that this is the watching hour; and that our supreme duty is to work until the day is done and darkness falls upon the fields; to watch until the hour is ended.

SIR WALTER RALEIGH (1552–1618).

HOME

When I speak of home, I speak of the place where those I love are gathered together; and if that place were a gipsy's tent or a barn, I should call it by the same good name notwithstanding.

CHARLES DICKENS (1812–70).

SERVICE

I expect to pass through this world but once. Any good work, therefore, any kindness, or any service I can render to any soul of man or animal, let me do it now! Let me not neglect or defer it, for I shall not pass this way again.

ANON.

THE RAINBOW

My heart leaps up when I behold
    A rainbow in the sky;
So was it when my life began;
So is it now I am a man;
So be it when I shall grow old,
    Or let me die!
The child is father of the man;
And I could wish my days to be
Bound each to each by natural piety.

W. WORDSWORTH (1770–1850).

ADDITIONAL POETRY FOR READING AND RECITATION

THE NATIONAL ANTHEM OF JAMAICA

Eternal Father, bless our land,
Guard us with Thy Mighty Hand,
Keep us free from evil powers,
Be our light through countless hours.
To our Leaders, Great Defender,
Grant true wisdom from above.
Justice, Truth, be ours forever,
Jamaica, land we love.
Jamaica, Jamaica, Jamaica, land we love.

Teach us true respect for all,
Stir response to duty's call,
Strengthen us the weak to cherish,
Give us vision lest we perish.
Knowledge send us, Heavenly Father,
Grant true wisdom from above.
Justice, Truth, be ours forever,
Jamaica, land we love.
Jamaica, Jamaica, Jamaica, land we love.

Hugh Sherlock

THE NATIONAL ANTHEM OF TRINIDAD AND TOBAGO

Forged from the love of liberty,
In the fires of hope and prayer,
With boundless faith in our destiny,

We solemnly declare:
Side by side we stand,
Islands of the blue Caribbean Sea,
This our native land, we pledge our lives to thee.
Here ev'ry creed and race find an equal place,
And may God bless our nation.
Here ev'ry creed and race find an equal place,
And may God bless our nation.

PATRICK S. CASTAGNE

WEST INDIAN POEMS

1. THE WEST INDIES

IN waters of purple and gold
Lie the islands beloved of the Sun,
And he touches them one by one,
As the beads of a rosary told,
When the glow of the dawn has begun,
And when to Eternity's fold
Time gathers the day that is done.

No rosary! Isles of the West,
Isles Antillean agleam,
But a necklace strung out on the breast
Of the sea breathing low in a dream,
In the trance of a passionate rest,
A rainbow afloat in its stream.

H. S. BUNBURY:
Songs and Ballads of Greater Britain.
(*By permission of J. M. Dent and Sons, Ltd.*)

2. THE JOYS OF JAMAICA

Empress of all the Spanish Main,
And Queen of Antillean isles,
What rival may dispute thy reign?
What traveller resist thy smiles?

By rivers sway the fern and palm
In winding valleys richly set,
While muffled in majestic calm
The forests stand unravished yet.

Here soars the massive mountain height,
The torrent foams along the glen,
There sweep and fade in golden light
Wide palms with sustenance for men.

And over and around all these
The buoyant trade wind softly blows,
It bears the balm of southern seas,
Yet cool its bracing current flows.

Heaven palpitates alive with stars,
Or moonlight holds the earth in trance,
Our soul resents its prison bars,
Our heart yet hungers for romance.

H. S. BUNBURY:
Songs and Ballads of Greater Britain.
(*By permission of J. M. Dent and Sons, Ltd.*)

TO A BUTTERFLY

Note.—Boys who delight in chasing butterflies should ponder over these pretty verses by Wordsworth. He gives us the proper point of view from which we ought to regard one of the loveliest of all created things.

I

STAY near me—do not take thy flight!
A little longer stay in sight!
Much converse do I find in thee,
Historian of my infancy!
Float near me; do not yet depart!
Dead times revive in thee:
Thou bring'st, gay creature as thou art,

A solemn image to my heart,
My father's family!

Oh! pleasant, pleasant were the days.
The time, when, in our childish plays,
My sister Emmeline and I
Together chased the butterfly!
A very hunter did I rush
Upon the prey:—with leaps and springs
I followed on from brake to bush;
But she, God love her, feared to brush
The dust from off its wings.

II

I've watched you now a full half-hour,
Self-poised upon that yellow flower;
And, little Butterfly! indeed
I know not if you sleep or feed.
How motionless!—not frozen seas
More motionless! and then
What joy awaits you, when the breeze
Hath found you out among the trees,
And calls you forth again!

This plot of orchard-ground* is ours;
My trees they are, my sister's flowers;
Here rest your wings when they are weary;
Here lodge as in a sanctuary!

Come often to us, fear no wrong;
Sit near us on the bough!
We'll talk of sunshine and of song,
And summer days when we were young:
Sweet childish days, they were as long
As twenty days are now.

William Wordsworth

* The poem was written in the poet's orchard.

A TRAGIC STORY

Note.—This humorous poem was originally written in German. Thackeray, the great novelist, adapted it into English.

THERE lived a sage in days of yore,
And he a handsome pigtail wore:
But wondered much and sorrowed more
   Because it hung behind him.

He mused upon this curious case,
And swore he'd change the pigtail's place,
And have it hanging at his face,
   Not dangling there behind him.

Says he, "The mystery I've found—
I'll turn me round" —he turned him round;
   But still it hung behind him.

Then round, and round, and out and in,
All day the puzzled sage did spin;
In vain—it mattered not a pin—
   The pigtail hung behind him.

And right, and left, and round about,
And up and down, and in and out,
He turned; but still the pigtail stout
   Hung steadily behind him.

And though his efforts never slack,
And though he twist, and twirl, and tack,
Alas! still faithful to his back
   The pigtail hangs behind him.

W. M. THACKERAY

THE NATIONAL ANTHEM OF BARBADOS

In plenty and in time of need,
When this fair land was young,
Our brave forefathers sowed the seed
From which our pride is sprung,
A pride that makes no wanton boast
Of what it has withstood,
That binds our hearts from coast to coast—
The pride of nationhood.

Chorus

We loyal sons and daughters
Do hereby make it known
These fields and hills beyond recall
Are now our very own.
We write our names on history's page
With expectations great,
Strict guardians of our heritage,
Firm craftsmen of our fate.

The Lord has been the people's guide
For past three hundred years.
With him still on the people's side
We have no doubts or fears.
Upward and onward we shall go,
Inspired, exulting, free,
And greater will our nation grow
In strength and unity.

IRVINE BURGIE

THE NATIONAL ANTHEM OF GUYANA

Dear land of Guyana, of rivers and plains,
Made rich by the sunshine and lush by the rains,
Set gem-like and fair between mountains and sea,
Your children salute you, dear land of the free.

Green land of Guyana, our heroes of yore,
Both bondsmen and free, laid their bones on your shore;
This soil so they hallowed, and from them are we,
All sons of one mother, Guyana the free.

Great land of Guyana, diverse though our strains,
We are born of their sacrifice, heirs of their pains,
And ours is the glory their eyes did not see—
One land of six peoples, united and free.

Dear land of Guyana, to you will we give
Our homage, our service, each day that we live.
God guard you, great Mother, and make us to be
More worthy our heritage—land of the free.

A. L. LUKER

THE HERITAGE

THE rich man's son inherits lands,
  And piles of brick and stones and gold;
And he inherits soft white hands,
  And tender flesh that fears the cold,
  Nor dares to wear a garment old;
A heritage, it seems to me,
One scarce would wish to hold in fee.

The rich man's son inherits cares:
  The bank may break, the factory burn;
A breath may burst his bubble shares,
  And soft white hands could hardly earn
  A living that would serve his turn;
A heritage, it seems to me,
One scarce would wish to hold in fee.

The rich man's son inherits wants:
  His stomach craves for dainty fare;
With sated heart he hears the pants
  Of toiling hands and brown arms bare,
  And wearies in his easy chair!

A heritage, it seems to me,
One scarce would wish to hold in fee.

What doth the poor man's son inherit?
  Stout muscles and a sinewy heart,
A sturdy frame, a hardier spirit,
  King of two hands, he does his part
  In every useful toil and art;
A heritage, it seems to me,
A king might wish to hold in fee.

What doth the poor man's son inherit?
  Wishes o'erjoyed with humble things,
A rank adjudged by toil-worn merit,
  Content that from employment springs
  A heart that in his labour sings;
A heritage, it seems to me,
A king might wish to hold in fee.

What doth the poor man's son inherit?
  A patience learned of being poor,
Courage, if sorrow come, to bear it,
  A fellow-feeling that is sure
  To make the outcast bless his door;
A heritage, it seems to me,
A king might wish to hold in fee.

O rich man's son! there is a toil
  That with all others level stands;
Large charity doth never soil,
  But only whiten, soft white hands—
  This is the best crop from thy lands;
A heritage, it seems to me,
Worth being rich to hold in fee.

O poor man's son! scorn not thy state;
There is worse weariness than thine
In merely being rich and great:
Toil only gives the soul to shine,
And makes rest fragrant and benign;
A heritage, it seems to me,
Worth being poor to hold in fee.

Both heirs to some six feet of sod,
Are equal in the earth at last;
Both children of the same dear God,
Prove title to your heirship vast
By record of a well-filled past;
A heritage, it seems to me,
Well worth a life to hold in fee.

JAMES RUSSELL LOWELL

THE SHIPS

FOR many a year I've watched the ships a-sailing to and fro,
The mighty ships, the little ships, the speedy and the slow;
And many a time I've told myself that some day I would go
Around the world that is so full of wonders.

The swift and stately liners, how they run without a rest!
The great three-masters, they have touched the East and told the West!
The monster burden-bearers—oh, they all have plunged and pressed
Around the world that is so full of wonders!

The shabby tramp that like a wedge is hammered through the seas,
The little brown-sailed brigantine that traps the lightest breeze—
Oh, I'd be well content to fare aboard the least of these
Around the world that is so full of wonders.

The things I've heard, the things I've read, the things I've dreamed might be,
The boyish tales, the old men's yarns—they will not pass from me;
I've heard, I've read, I've dreamed. . . . But all the time I've longed to *see*—
Around the world that is so full of wonders.

So year by year I watch the ships a-sailing to and fro,
The ships that come as strangers and the ships I've learned to know. . . .
Folk smile to hear an old man say that *some* day he will go
Around the world that is so full of wonders.

J. J. BELL

(By kind permission of the Author.)